Horseshoeing for Horseowners

by

David A. Duquette

Cover Photo by Robert R. Lieske

Library of Congress Number 88-80060
ISBN Number 0-945782-00-4

Published by
H. F. H. Publications
P.O. Box 81
La Grande, Oregon 97850

DISCLAIMER OF LIABILITIES

<u>WARNING:</u>

The pictures, descriptions and procedures in this book have been developed with the safety of the horseowner foremost in mind. However, the dispositions of animals are unpredictable and varied and the Author assumes no liability, express or implied, for injury or death to any person or animal resulting from shoeing horses while following the instructions in this book.

INTRODUCTION

This book has grown out of a need I discovered while I was a practicing farrier. Customers were constantly asking what work they could do on their own horses when I was not around. I began a Horseshoeing for Horseowners class at various colleges in the Northwest. These classes demonstrated the proper techniques and procedures for trimming and shoeing for horseowners. As the classes grew and the demand spread it became evident that a book to go along with the class was needed. This book is my attempt to help horse owners learn what is involved in shoeing and what they can and cannot do on their own. This is not a book to teach people to become horseshoers, only to instruct horseowners on how to work on their own horses.

My feeling is that there are many things that can be done by an owner depending on talent, desire and ability. I like to compare it to automobile maintenence. Almost everyone can change a tire (pull shoes), most can do a minor tune-up (barefoot trim) and a few can do major overhauls (shoeing). This book will give the horseowner the knowledge to do what his/her ability will allow.

At the very least, this book will help make the horseowner a better consumer. The horseowner will be able to know the principles involved in horseshoeing and allow the horseowner to intelligently assess what is being done to the horse. At the very most, this book will allow the horseowner to do most of the trimming and shoeing on their horse with a farrier follow-up once in a while. The majority of horseowners will fall somewhere in between these extremes.

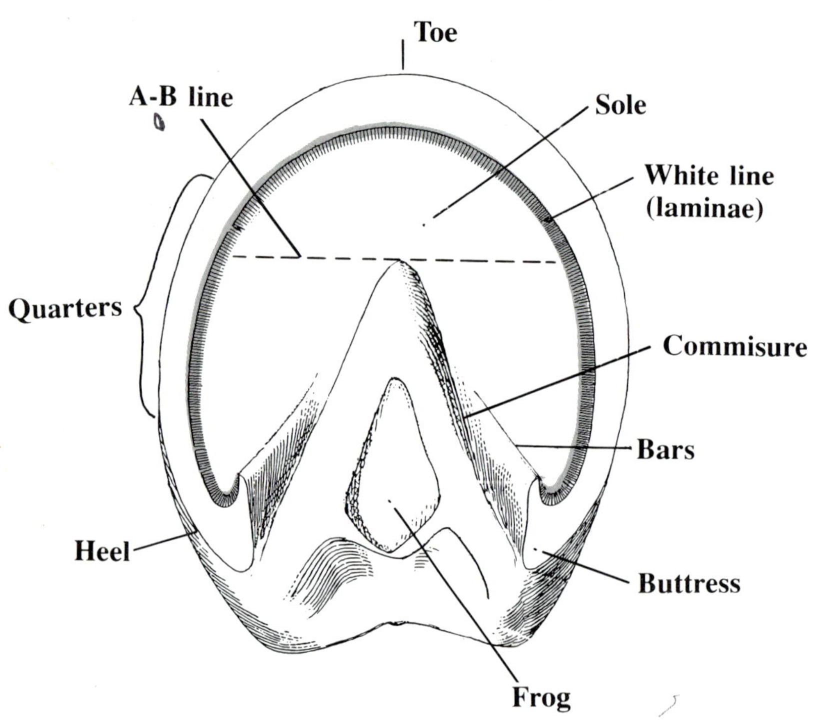

Toe
A-B line
Sole
White line
(laminae)
Quarters
Commisure
Bars
Heel
Buttress
Frog

ANATOMY

Any person working on a horse's foot must have at least a fundamental understanding of the anatomy (structure) and physiology (function) of the horse's lower leg and foot. There are many excellent books on anatomy which one can study. The discussion presented here is limited to the most simple principles needed to help a person understand what is involved in trimming or shoeing a horse properly.

Shoeing a horse, at best, is a necessary evil. When more of the horse's hoof wall is worn off than the normal growth of the wall can replace, the horse needs shoes. Horseshoeing is harmful in many ways. Among these are: the driving of nails and subsequent holes in the hoof; unnatural elongation of the hoof wall by adding a shoe; adding weight on the foot; limiting expansion of the foot; and lifting the foot and frog off the ground. The following pages will help the horseowner understand the workings of the foot and how to trim and shoe, based on the proper function of the foot.

Structure- The hoof is made up of five structures.

The *"hoof wall"* is the outside covering of the hoof. It is the part seen when the horse is in a standing position. The hoof wall varies in thickness from heel to toe. On an average saddle horse, the wall at the toe is 3/8" to 1/2" thick and about half that at the quarters. The wall is thickest at the toe where the wear is the greatest. As the horse picks his foot up to move, the toe is subjected to wear as the foot breaks over. The reduction in thickness at the quarters allows the wall to be flexible and expand with pressure. This helps absorb the tremendous concussion of the foot striking the ground.

The *"periople"* is the varnish-like covering of the hoof wall that helps protect and keep moisture in the hoof.

The *"sole"* covers the ground surface of the foot and protects the sensitive structures inside. The sole is concave in relation to the ground and is more so in a hind foot. The sole is usually 3/8" thick where is unites with the white line and somewhat thinner toward the point of the frog. On a barefoot horse, the sole tends to flake off on its own. However, when the horse has shoes on, the sole will build up. This must be taken into account when trimming. In other words, when a horse has been barefoot, less, if any, sole will be pared away than when a horse has had shoes on.

The *"frog"* is the wedge shaped projection located between the heels. The frog also helps dissipate concussion (along with the foot expansion) and has a non-slipping function to help stabilize the foot. The frog also is very elastic. It helps circulate blood up the horse's leg by compressing the plantor cushion which is full of blood. The frog must be allowed to make contact with the ground for these functions to operate as intended.

The *"white line"* is the outer portion of the laminae system that unites the outer hoof wall to the inner structures of the foot. It is usually pale yellow in color and about 1/8" in width. The white line is made up of many interlocking laminae, the ends of which can be seen.

The foot contains two bones and half of another. The coffin bone is extremely porous and is the bone that gives the outer hoof its shape. The porosity of the coffin bone allows it to be well supplied with nerves and permits tendons, ligaments, and collateral cartilages a strong attachment. The navicular bone is located at the junction of the coffin and short pastern bones. It provides a surface for the deep flexor tendon to slide over when flexing the foot. Although not a part of the foot, the long pastern bone is important in this discussion. The angle formed by the long and short pastern bones is the angle used when deciding at what angle to trim the hoof. (Refer to diagram on trimming.)

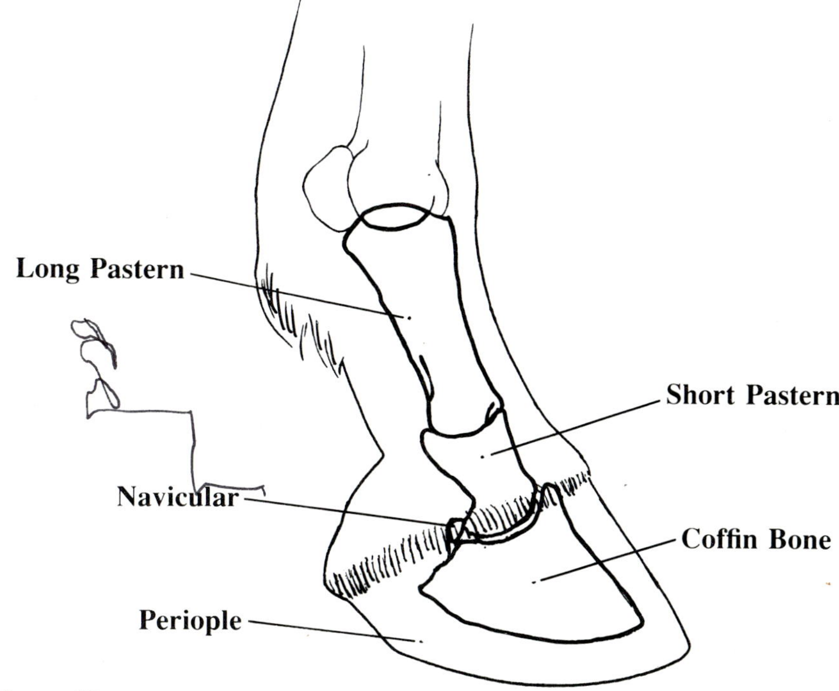

Diagram #1.

The horse's foot is a complex and highly efficient structure. It provides supporting, anti-concussion, circulatory and non-slipping functions. The foot is made up of bones, ligaments, tendons, elastic structures, blood vessels and nerves.

The weight of the horse is supported by the bones, ligaments and tendons of the foot and leg. The weight is supported and transferred from the hoof to the body through the various bones, ligaments and tendons. As weight is applied to the leg, several things happen to absorb the concussion. The bones slide over each other slightly. The pastern sinks and the hoof expands. The frog makes contact with the ground and pushes up on the plantor cushion which then spreads the lateral cartilages. The heels expand with contact with the ground. Simultaneously, the blood in the various venous plexus (plantor cushion, lateral cartilages, etc.) forms a "hydraulic cushion", while the elasticity of the white line, sole and wall also help spread the shock throughout the entire foot.

It is important to allow the frog to have contact with the ground when trimming. If the frog is kept from the ground, through cutting it out or excessive heel caulks on shoes, the plantor cushion will sink downward when the foot makes contact instead of being forced to expand by the frog. If this occurs, the lateral cartilages will be pulled inward and the hoof will contract instead of expand. This will prevent the foot from performing its major function of shock absorbtion and could cause lameness or injury to the horse.

The heels of the foot should not be prevented from expanding when the foot makes contact with the ground. This can be caused by excessive cutting of the heels in trimming, by nails being driven too far back in the foot or through improper fitting or shaping of the shoe. If the heels can not expand the plantor cushion and lateral cartilages will not expand as they should, thereby reducing the absorbing function of each.

===================== NOTES =====================

TOOLS

There are many horseshoeing tools which a professional farrier will need but which a horseowner would find unnecessary. This section will list the tools most generally needed for home horseshoeing. Some adequate substitutes will be mentioned. It has been the author's experience that the best tools that can be purchased, although more expensive in the beginning, will last virtually forever and allow the horseowner to do the best job.

Hoof Nipper - Hoof nippers are used to remove excess hoof wall. This is the most important tool needed by a horseowner who is going to work on his/her horses. Without a good quality hoof nipper it will be almost impossible for a beginner to cut the excess hoof wall level enough for a shoeing. Nippers come in 12", 13", 14" and 15" sizes. The 15" nipper will prove satisfactory for most saddle horses and owners.

Hoof nippers also come in various head styles. The only style to consider for the use intended in this book is the flat design. Other basic styles available (which should not be used) are: the overlap style where the cutting edge slides under one branch and the pointed edge where the branches meet but have a bevel on both sides. It is extremely hard to get a good level cut with these types of nippers. Since the quality of the trimming or shoeing job depends on the quality of the nippering job, the horseowner should get the best nipper available.

Hoof Knife - The hoof knife is used to cut away dead sole from the bottom of the hoof, trim parts of the frog for hygienic reasons and to remove foreign materials from the foot.

Knives come in narrow and wide blade styles and are 2 1/2 to 3" long. Hoof knives come in left-handed and right-handed styles and also double edge.

The most common one in use is the wide blade single edge. The double edge knife is not really practical since much of the work done with the hoof knife is done with one thumb pushing on the blade. With a double edge knife this can be uncomfortable. The wide blade is generally used since it will last longer when being sharpened as there is more blade to begin with. Most farriers would have a couple of knives, a wide blade for everyday hoof paring and a thin blade for hard to get corners, exploring absesses, etc. The horse owner will only need one knife to do the work required. The knife should always be kept sharp and this is best accomplished with a round fine-cut file.

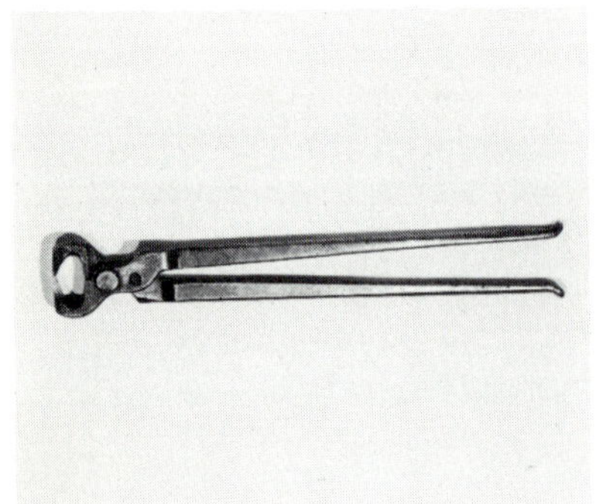

Fig 1. Hoof Nipper - note the flat cutting edge

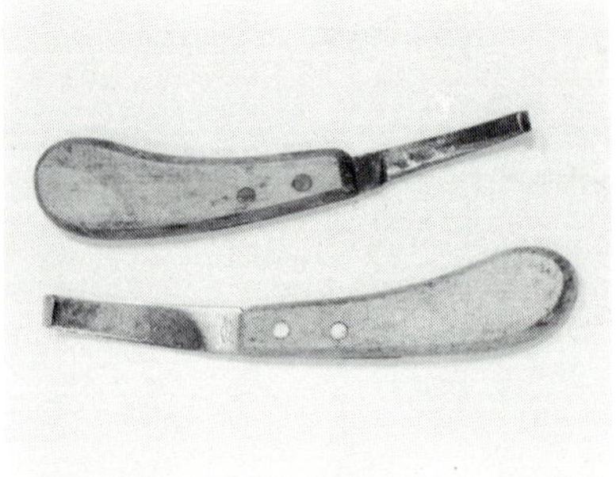

Fig 2. Hoof Knives - (bottom knife right handed wide blade, top is a left handed narrow blade

Horsehoeing Rasp - The rasp is used to level the bearing surface of the hoof wall after the excess wall of the foot has been removed with the nippers and to remove abnormal flares from the hoof. The rasp can be used to remove burrs under the nail before clinching, to smooth the clinches and to finish the hoof.

The most popular rasp is the 14" double extra-thin tonged rasp. This is a rasp with a coarse side for rapid hoof removal and a fine side for finishing the hoof and as a clinching rasp. The rasp should have a wooden handle for safety.

Clinch Cutter - The clinch cutter is used to remove the clinches when pulling old shoes off. A typical clinch cutter has two parts, the blade and the point. The blade is approximately 1" wide and is used to slide under the clinches and to cut or raise them when hit with the shoeing hammer. The point is used to open up a nail hole on the shoe if it has been closed while shaping the shoe. The point can also be used to raise a nail head from the shoe crease sufficiently to allow it to be pulled out with nail nippers or pulloffs. When looking for or making a clinch cutter (out of leaf spring) it is advisable to bevel only one side of the blade to make it easier to slide under the clinch. Clinch cutters also work better if the blade is a little dull. This helps prevent cutting the hoof wall when lifting the clinches.

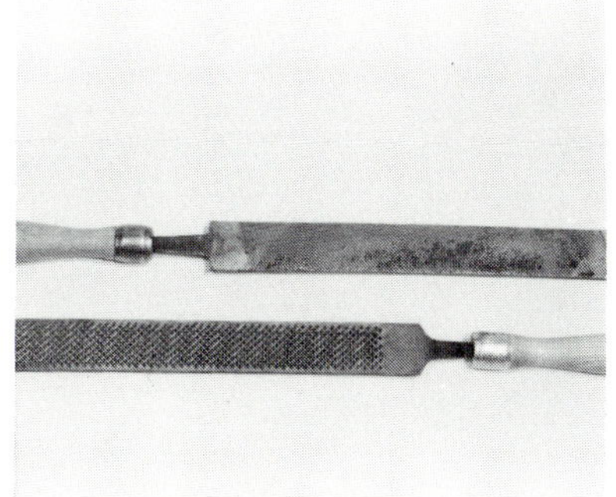

Fig 3. Horseshoeing Rasp - Notice the fine and rough sides

Fig 4. Clinch cutters

Shoe Pull Offs - Pull offs are used to remove old shoes by sliding the jaws between the shoe and the hoof. Sometimes old hoof nippers can be used for this purpose if the blades are dull. Some pull offs have serrated edges on the outside which can allow them to be used as shoe spreaders. This can help beginners get the proper expansion in the shoe at the heels.

Shoeing Hammer - Also called driving hammers, shoeing hammers are used to drive nails into the hoof, strike the clinch cutter when removing shoes and bend nails over after being driven through the hoof. Driving hammers come usually in 10 oz., 14 oz., and 16 oz. weights. The 14 or 10 oz. sizes are adequate for saddle horses.

When choosing a driving hammer, look for one in which the striking face is as large as possible since this will facilitate driving nails for beginners. A light carpenter's hammer, no heavier than 16 oz., will work. However, remember it is better to have a hammer a little light than one that is too heavy. If the hammer is too heavy, the horse might be sensitive to the pounding and the soft shoeing nails will tend to bend and warp as they are being driven into the hoof. Shoeing hammers also come with wooden and fiberglass handles. Either one will give adequate service.

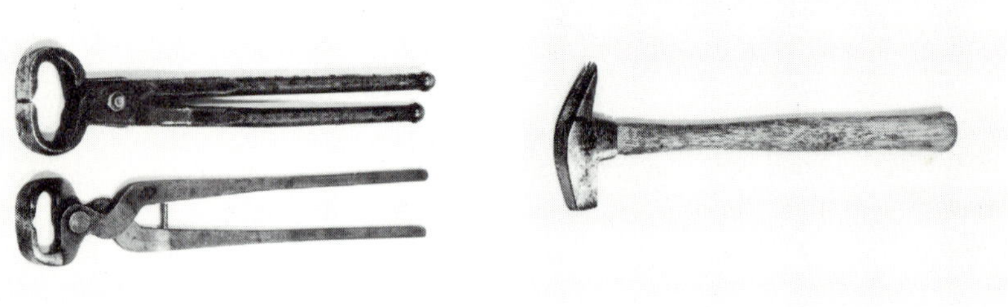

Fig 5. Two different styles of shoe pull offs

Fig 6. 14oz. driving hammer

Clinchers - Sometimes called clinching tongs or alligators, clinchers are used to finish off the nail clinches. They bend over the nail and seat it into the hoof wall. Good clinchers will do much to improve the shoeing job since good clinches are one of the main components of a good shoeing job.

Clinchers come in several styles. The one needed for most saddle horses is the alligator clincher. Other types are the farrier clincher and the gooseneck clincher.

Nail Nippers - Nail nippers are used to cut off turned over nails in preparation for clinching and to help pull nails out of a shoe. Almost any type of nail nippers will function satisfactorily.

Clinch Block - The clinch block is used primarily to tighten the clinches in preparation for the clinchers. It is not an absolutely necessary tool since the same function can be performed with the side of a rasp or pull offs. However they are useful to have and can be made out of any block of metal. A protruding lip for the hand to rest in is a help.

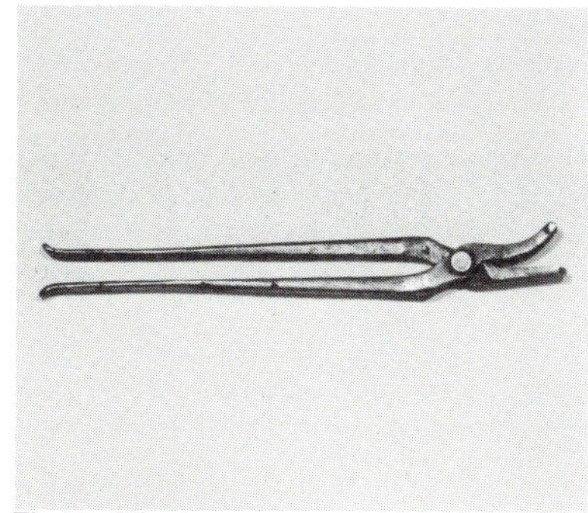

Fig 7. Clinchers

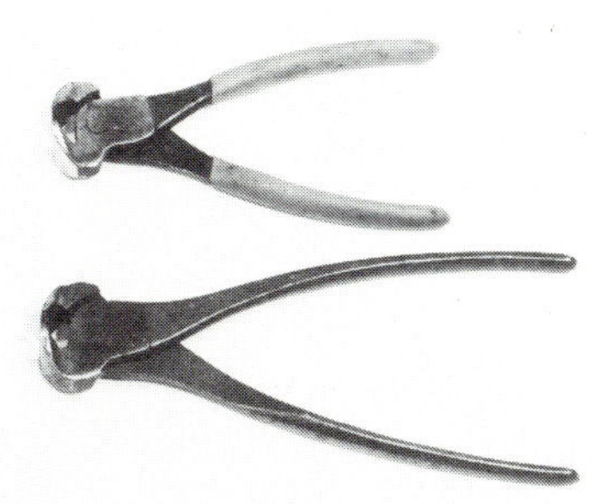

Fig 8. Two styles of nail nippers

Shaping Hammer - The shaping hammer is used to shape the shoe to the desired shape on the anvil. It generally has a rounded and a flat surface head. The flat side is used for shaping while the rounded edge can be used when leveling the shoe. The shaping hammer generally weighs between 1 1/2 to 2 1/2 pounds. Any hammer (ball peen for example) weighing about 2 pounds will do an adequate job. Do not use a hammer heavier than 2 1/2 lbs. as it will tend to warp the shoe when striking it.

Fig 9. Home made clinch block

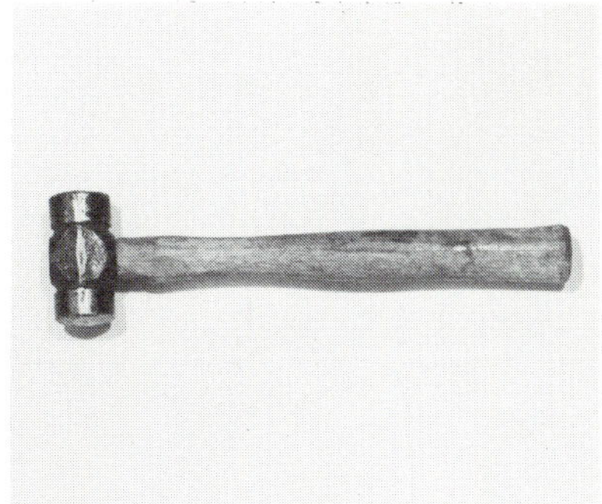

Fig 10. Shaping hammer

Shoeing Apron- The shoeing apron is worn to protect the legs from protruding nails and to save wear and tear on the clothes. Although it is a nice accessory to have, it is not absolutely necessary. Any old heavy duty pants will suffice.

Foot Stand - The foot stand is used to place the horse's foot on when clinching nails, finishing the foot or any other time the top of the foot is worked on. This tool, while not absolutely necessary, as the foot can be brought forward on the horseowner's lap or leg, is a tool that should be used whenever possible. Most horses seem to adjust to it rapidly. It does take quite a strain off the horseowner's body and makes the job of working on the horse much more tolerable. Stands can be fancy works of art or as simple as the agitator blade from a broken washing machine. The stand needs a center piece approximately 16-18" high and 2" in diameter. This center pole should be mounted on a wide base to give soome support and to prevent the stand from being pushed over from the weight of the horse. The easiest kind to make and also the most stable is one made out of an old disc harrow and piece of 1 1/2" pipe. The pipe is welded to the middle of the harrow. Most local welding shops can make one of these.

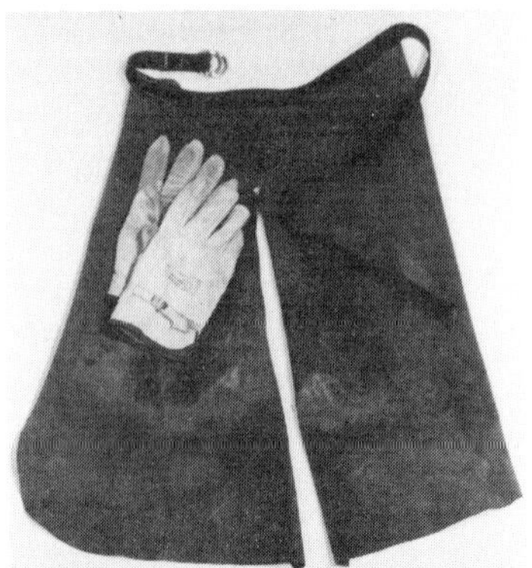

Fig 11. Shoeing apron and leather gloves

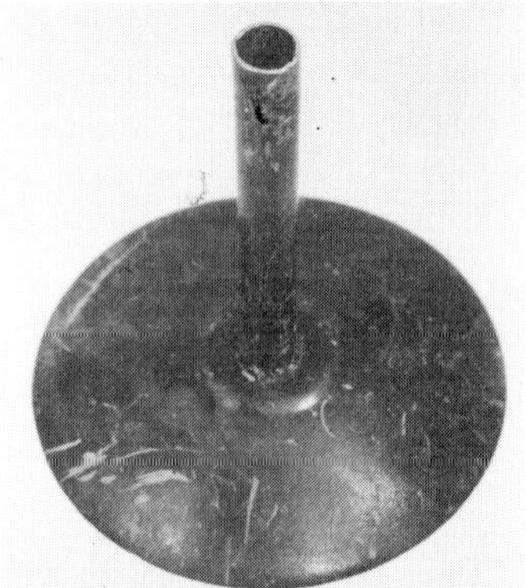

Fig 12. Foot stand made from disc harrow

Anvil- The anvil is used to shape each shoe before nailing it in the foot. It is really impossible to shape a shoe without an anvil. While a horseshoeing anvil is different in some respects from a blacksmith's anvil, either will work. The chief differences are that the horseshoeing anvil has a longer horn and a clip horn for pulling clips when hot shoeing.

(Author's note: If the horseowner doesn't have an anvil or access to one and is going to buy one, these are the points for which to look. It should be at least 50 lbs. in weight and generally not more than 150 lbs. The heel of the anvil should be shallow enough to allow a branch of the shoe to slide into the hardy hole. In addition, there are several styles of new anvils that can be purchased for approximately $1.00 a pound. While adequate for most horseowners, it should be noted that the steel used is very soft and will not stand up to heavy use.)

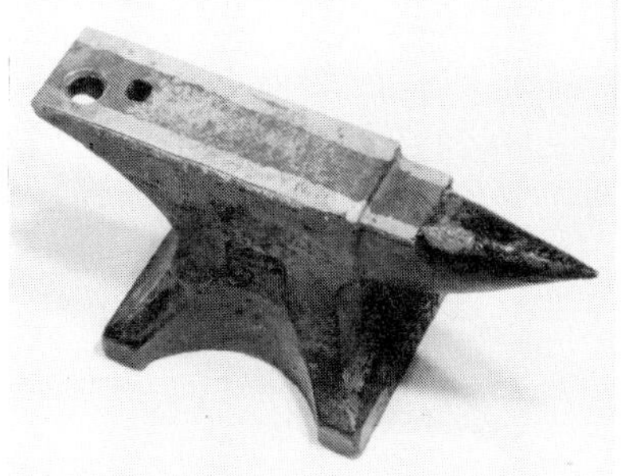

Fig 13. Blacksmith anvil with a hole drilled to allow branch of shoe to pass through

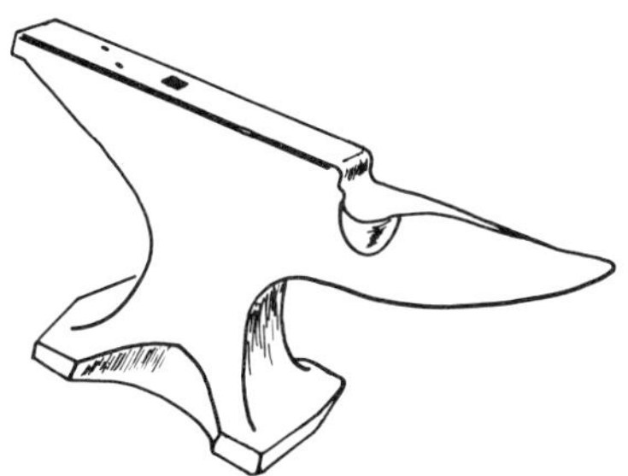

Diagram 2. Shoeing anvil

It is recommended that not all the tools mentioned be purchased immediately. Not all horseowners have the inclination or ability to shoe their horse. However the majority should be able to trim. Therefore the tools you buy first should be the ones needed for trimming. These tools are the hoof nippers, hoof knife, footstand and a rasp. This should cost approximately $50-60 (without the footstand). A foot stand should be able to be made at a local welding shop for $5-10.

If after trimming the horse a couple of times you decide that shoeing is within your abilities, then the shoeing tools (hammer, shaping hammer, alligator clinchers, apron, clinch cutter, nail nippers) can be purchased. These tools can be bought for an additional

$125-150. The cost can be kept down by making some of these or buying them used. However it is recommended that the tools be bought new from a reputable dealer.

The anvil will be the most expensive item purchased. A new anvil will cost $3-4 a pound. However a used anvil can sometimes be found at garage sales, auctions, etc. for $1 to $1.50 a pound. A used anvil is more than adequate for the purpose intended here.

NOTES

CLEANING THE FOOT

Any time any work is to be done on the hoof, it must be cleaned. Wet mud can be cleared off with a towel or cloth. Dry mud or dirt can be scraped off with the edge of the rasp. Once the outside of the foot is cleaned, the foot can be picked up and the bottom cleaned out. This can be done with either a hoof pick or the dull side of the hoof knife.

> *Step 1-* Insert the pick (or other tool) into the material at the rear of the commisure (between the frog and buttress of the heel) and push the pick through to the toe.

> *Step 2-* Repeat this procedure on the other commissure.

> *Step 3-* Pull the pick around the toe inside the shoe or hoof wall.

Proper cleaning of the foot is an important hygenic procedure and should be done anytime the horseowner is doing anything with the horse. Not only will it do much to prevent disease but the owner can check for any foreign objects which could cause lameness. Regular cleaning of the foot also will help train the horse to stand for future shoeing and will help condition the horseowner also.

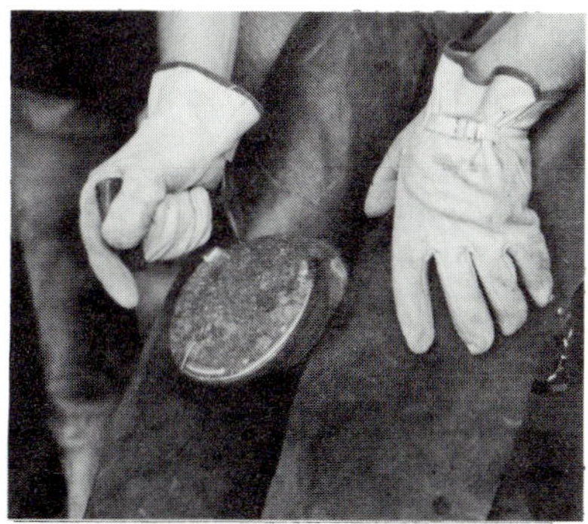

Fig 14. Put foot in shoeing position

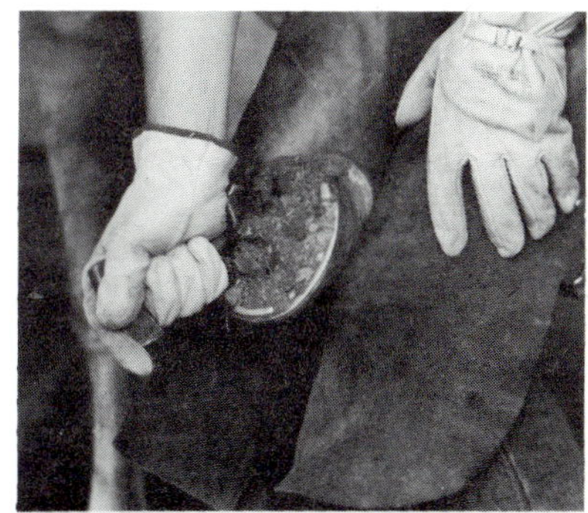

Fig 15. Insert pick in one commisure - push to the toe

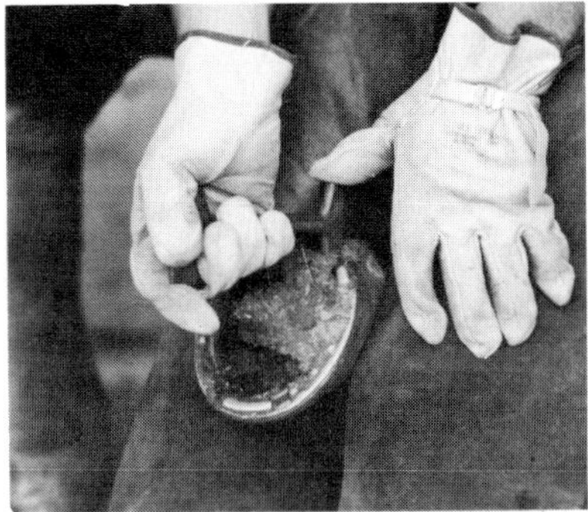

Fig 16. Insert pick in other commisure

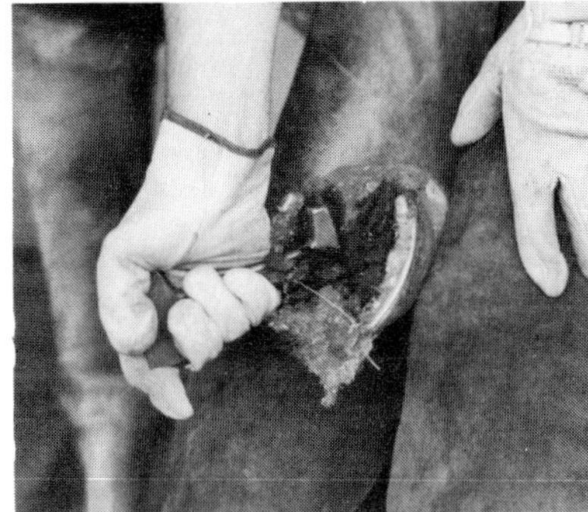

Fig 17. Push through to toe

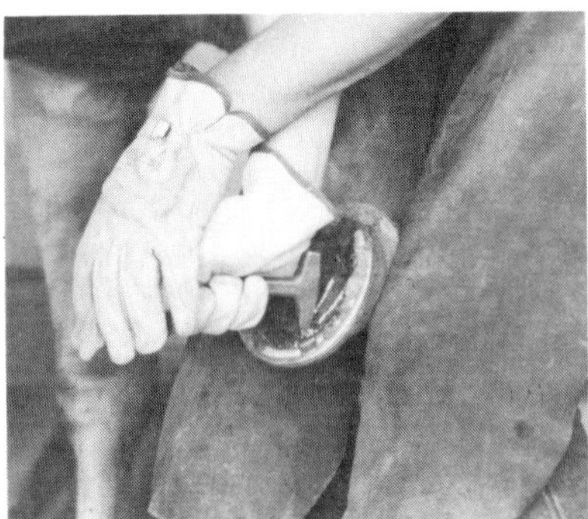

Fig 18. Run the pick around the toe

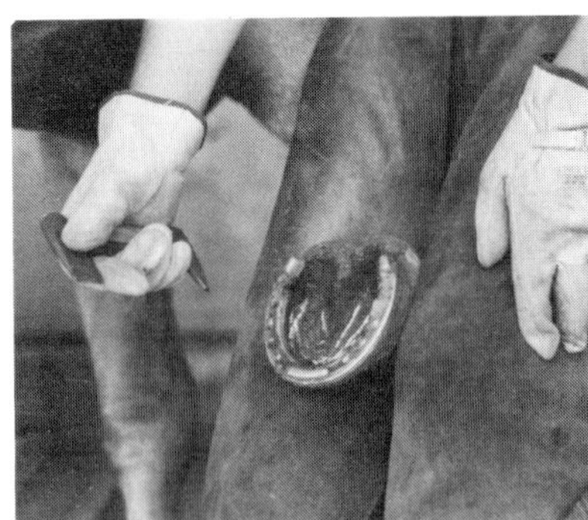

Fig 19. Cleaned out foot

================================ NOTES ================================

HORSE HANDLING

The assumption being made in this section is that the horse being worked with is gentle and has been shod many times before. If the horse is young, fractious or otherwise will not stand for shoeing, it is recommended that the horseowner seek professional help. It is hard enough to do a good shoeing job when the horse will cooperate and nearly impossible when the horse will not.

The area in which the work is to be done must be free from all debris and objects which could "spook" or injure the horse. The area should be one with which the horse is familiar and away from other activities which would distract the horse. The ideal area should be level, dry, protected from the elements, and with plenty of room in which to move around.

Whenever possible the horse should be held by a helper or a friend. Many horses will be easier to work with when a person is holding it. Besides, companionship will also help the horseowner--misery loves company.

When it is not possible to have a helper hold the horse, it must be tied. A strong halter and tie rope is a must. The halter should fit the horse properly, that is, not be too tight or too loose. In addition, the halter should be made out of nylon or similar material. The rope should be one inch thick and made of cotton. Tie the horse to a strong immoveable object with a halter and rope that will not break. Nothing is worse than a horse that has successfully broken free in the past. If a horse gets the notion that it can break free, nothing will be able to hold it.

The ideal way to tie a horse is to crosstie. Crosstying is done by tying a rope on either side of the halter and then tying the ropes 8 to 10 feet apart. This method of tying is safest for both the horseowner and horse while working.

HOOF HANDLING

Hoof handling is the hard part of shoeing or trimming the horse. If the horseowner can learn how to make the horse comfortable while working on the hoof, the job will be much easier. The tendency of most beginners is to tire easily and forget the proper position. It is much better to have the horseowner uncomfortable than the horse. If the horse is not comfortable it may act up, pull its foot away or lean. All of these actions will make it harder to do a good job. The horseowner should practice the positions and develop the muscles necessary to get along with the horse rather than expect the horse to get along with a tired horseowner. If the horseowner gets tired or cramped, he should put the foot down and rest. The horse will be easier to work with and hence make the job of shoeing and trimming easier for the horseowner.

Front Foot

Step 1- Slowly approach the horse from the head. Touch the horse on the upper neck near the mane. Rub and/or pat him. This not only establishes contact with the horse, but also lets it know you are there and gives you a clue as to how the horse might react to you.

Step 2- Facing the rear of the horse slide the near hand down the leg from the shoulder. Stop in the middle of the cannon bone and squeeze the horse between the flexor tendon and bone. Squeezing here causes the leg to relax much like a reflex action. At the same time pick up the foot with the off hand. You may need to lean into the horse's shoulder to cause it to shift its weight at the same time.

Step 3- Immediately fold the leg up.

Fig 20. Establish contact with the horse

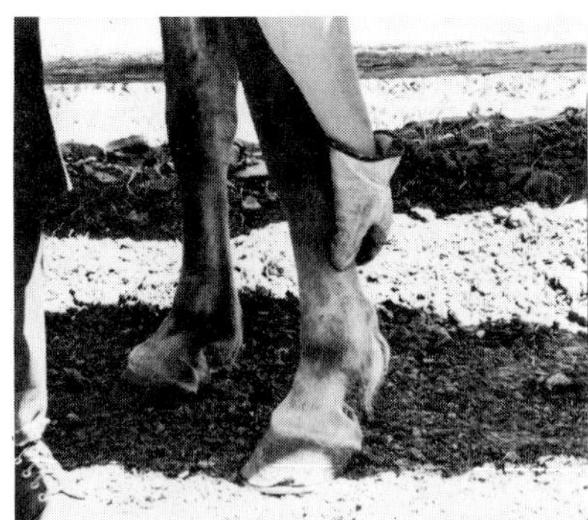

Fig 21. Squeeze the space between the flexor tendon and the cannon bone

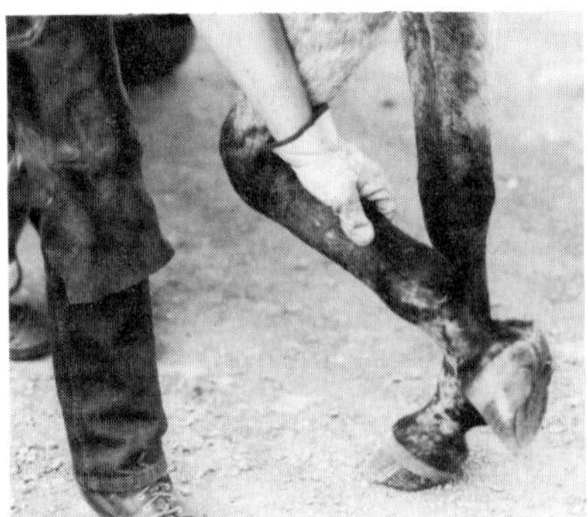

Fig 22. Fold the leg up with the off hand

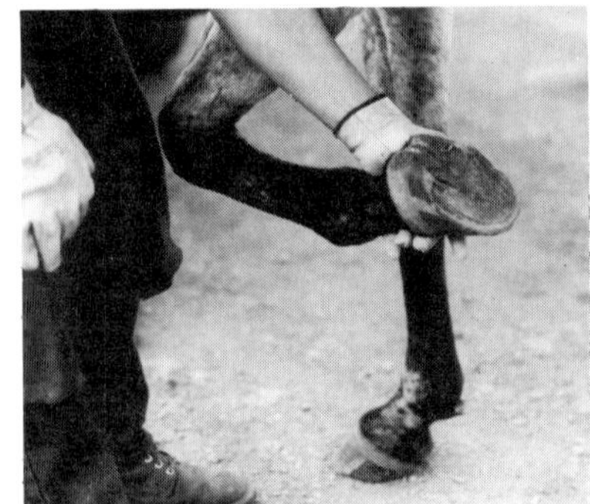

Fig 23. Change hands holding the foot

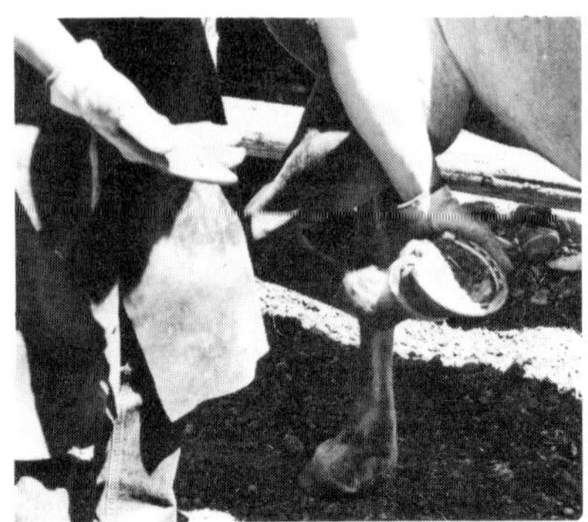

Fig 24. This is called the "home" position

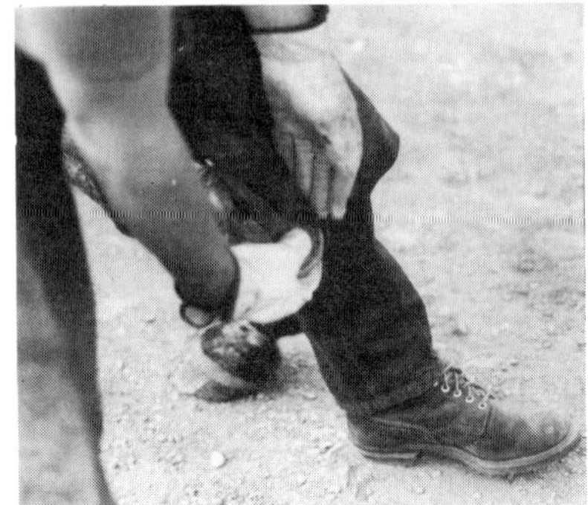

Fig 25. Slide foot between your legs

Step 4- Change hands holding the foot. This is called the "home" position.

Step 5- Slide the foot between your legs by bringing your near leg forward and passing the foot between your legs.

Step 6- Position the foot slightly above your knees. Be sure enough foot is sticking out so you can work on it. *(The foot should actually be held in the pastern area by your leg, slightly above the knee).*

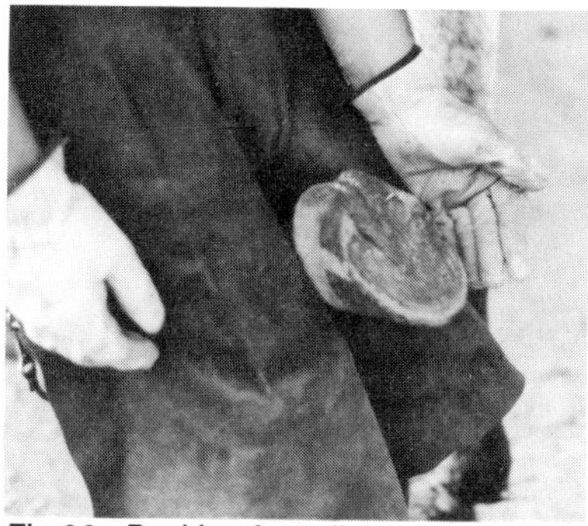

Fig 26. Position foot slightly above your knees

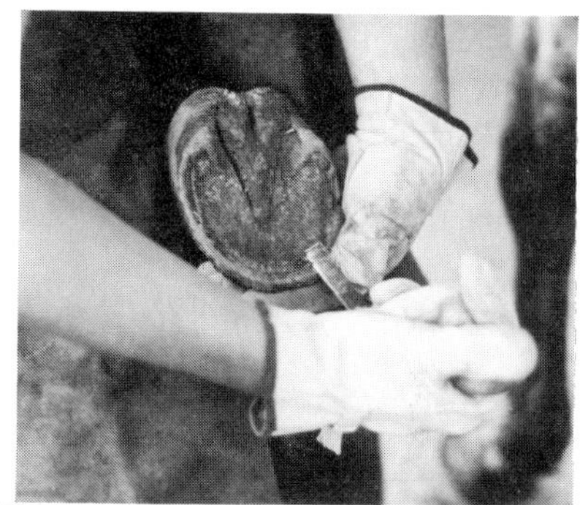

Fig 27. Be sure enough of foot is sticking out

Step 7- Turn your toes in and heels out while crouching slightly. Try to keep your back straight and bend at the knees. It is very important to keep yourself turned slightly into the horse. The horse's front leg is limited in its mobility to the side. The shoulder joint does not allow much movement to the side. What will happen as the horseowner gets tired is that, unconsciously, the body will begin to drift out. This puts pressure on the horse's shoulder joint and the horse will begin to act up, not out of meanness but out of pain. Keep good position and the horse will tend to cooperate.

Front Foot Forward

The front foot must be brought forward to finish clinching the nails, to shape the foot and to remove flares.

Holding the foot in the forward position can be extremely dangerous and awkward. For this reason a foot stand should always be used.

> *Step 1-* Place the foot stand in front of the horse.

> *Step 2-* Place the foot in the home position as described in the previous section.

> *Step 3-* Bring the foot forward and place it on the foot stand. The stand may need to be moved from side-to-side or front-to-back to allow the horse to be comfortable.

> *Step 4-* Stand to the outside of the horse's leg and slightly behind. One foot may need to be placed on the base of the foot stand to help stabilize it.

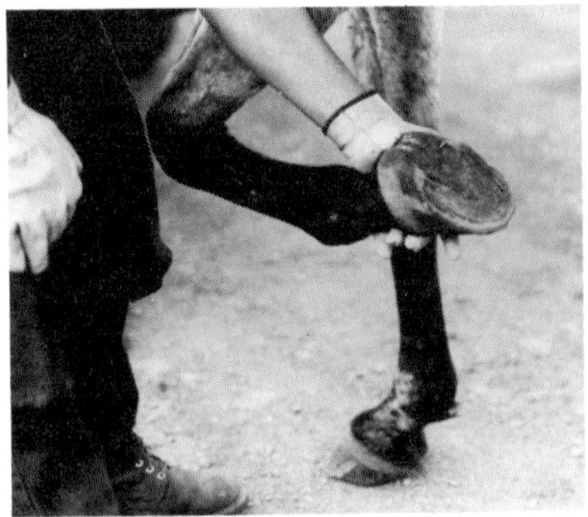

Fig 28. Place foot in home position

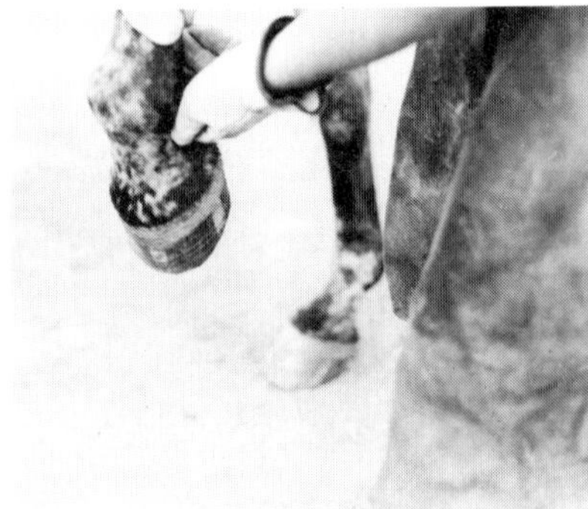

Fig 29. Bring foot forward

Fig 30. Place on foot stand

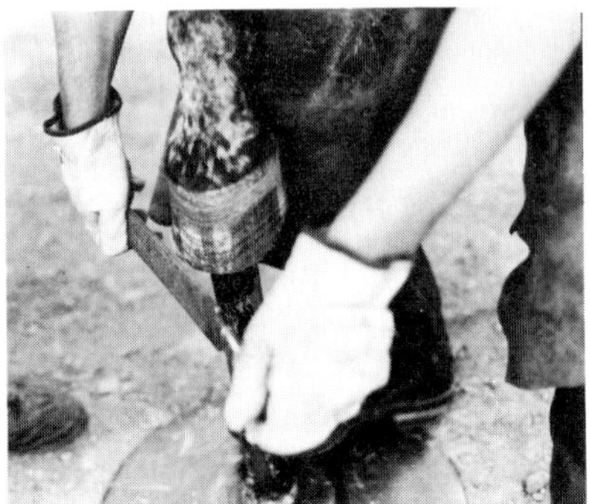

Fig 31. Stand to outside and behind foot

Rear Foot

Step 1- Approach the horse from the head. Pat the horse on the neck to let it know you are there. Slide the near hand along the back of the horse to its hip.

Step 2- Slide the near hand down the back of the horse's leg to the middle of the cannon bone--midway between the hock and fetlock.

Step 3- Push with the body and raise the leg with the near hand. Always remain close to the horse. Your back should be in contact with the horse's belly.

Step 4- Bring the off hand to the foot and grasp the toe, folding it up into itself.

Step 5- Step towards the rear of the horse with the off leg. Bring your near leg under the horse's leg at the cannon bone.

Step 6- Slowly "walk" the horse's leg out until you feel the horse relax.

Fig 32. Slide near hand down the back to the hip

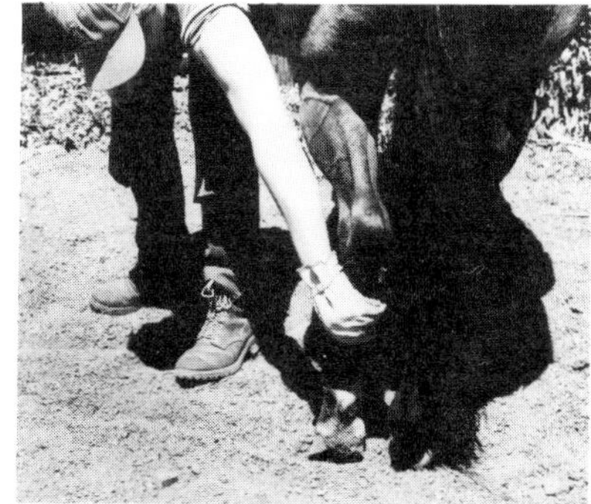

Fig 33. Slide hand to middle of cannon bone

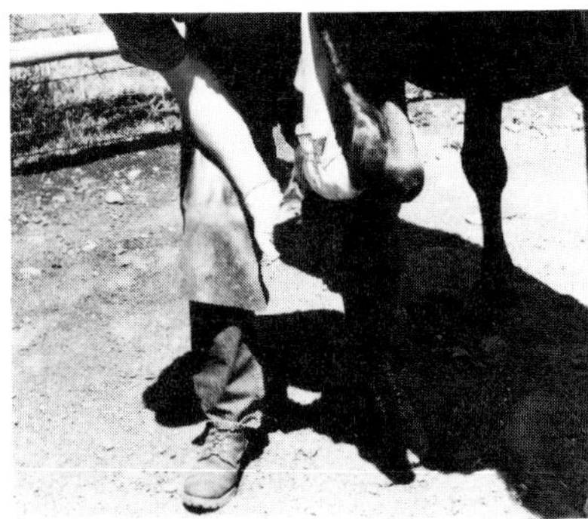

Fig 34. Raise the leg and grasp the toe

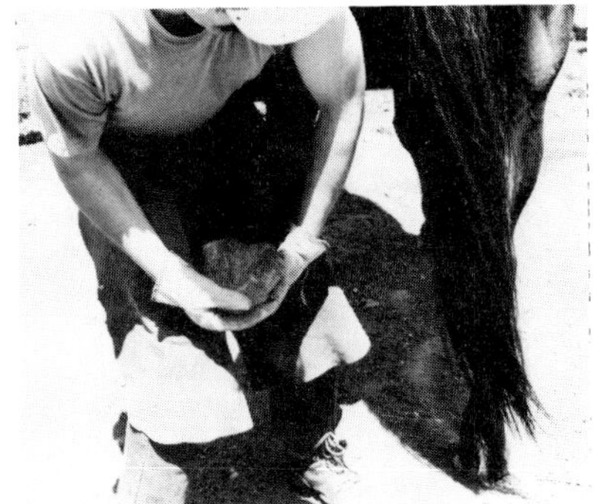

Fig 35. Slowly walk the horse out

Fig 36. The horse's leg should rest across your hip

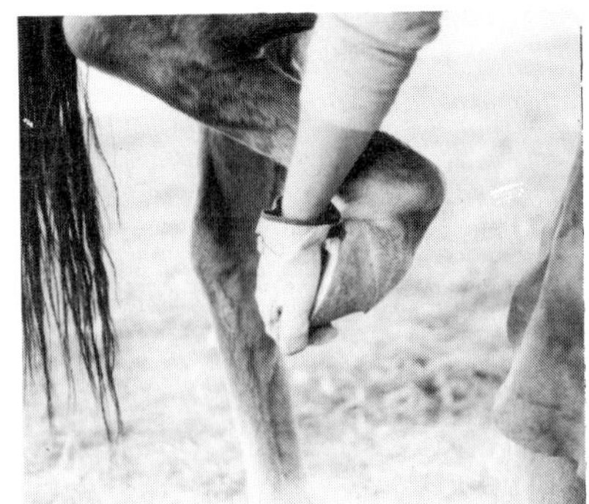

Fig 37. Home position

Step 7- The horse's leg should rest across your thigh with the foot resting on your outside knee. Point your toes inward, spread your heels and crouch. Let your legs do the work. This is the basic position. Some horses will be more comfortable stretched out behind while others will be more comfortable up close. You should be able to tell when the horse is comfortable as he will relax.

Home Position

With the horse's foot in your lap, grasp the toe with the near hand and step back into the horse--your back against the horse's belly. This is the "home position". This is a good position to go to if the horse begins to act up.

Bringing   Rear   Foot   Forward

Step 1- Place foot stand under the horse.

Step 2- Bring the rear foot into the home position as described previously.

Step 3- Bring the foot forward by grasping the leg in the middle of the cannon bone as the body is turned to face the front of the horse.

Step 4- Place the foot on the foot stand.

Step 5- Adjust the position of the stand according to

Fig 38. Place foot stand under the horse

Fig 39. Place foot in home position

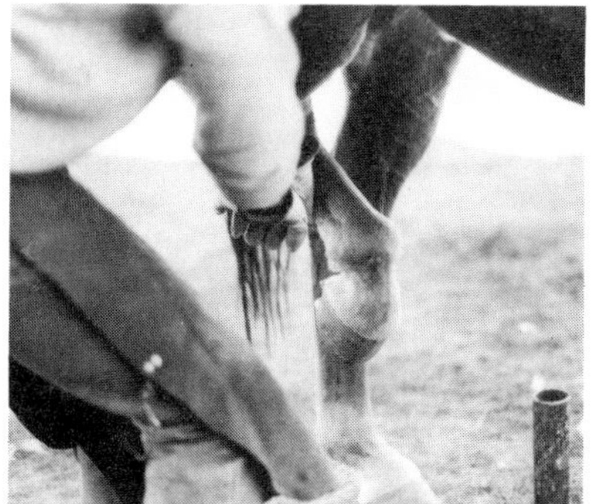
Fig 40. Turn to face the front of the horse

Fig 41. Bring foot forward

Fig 42. Place foot on stand

Fig 43. Take position to the rear and outside of foot

the horse's comfort.

Step 6- Take your position to the rear and outside of the horse's foot.

NOTES

TRIMMING - BAREFOOT

Trimming the horse's foot to go barefoot is the one thing that almost all horseowners can accomplish with a little practice. With regular and proper trimming, most horses can be used sensibly without having shoes on.

Trimming to go barefoot is done differently than when trimming to prepare the foot for a shoe. Generally the difference is in the amount of excess hoof wall cut off and the rounding of the edge of the hoof wall. When leaving a horse barefoot, more hoof wall (approximately 1/8" more) needs to be left, to act as a shoe. The sharp outer edge of the hoof wall will also need to be well rounded to prevent chipping of the hoof. When a horse is barefoot it actually helps to strengthen the hoof. At least 2-3 months of the year the horse should be left without shoes. While the hoof is barefoot, attention needs to be given to the condition of the hoof. Every 2 weeks or so the rasp should be taken to the hoof wall to keep it rounded.

The advantages to the horseowner in trimming the horse's feet are numerous. The horseowner can give frequent attention to any problems. If a crack or split is developing, prompt attention can prevent any damage. It is better to trim frequently if only with the rasp than to wait too long and have a problem occur because of an excessively long hoof. With young colts, frequent and proper trimming can prevent some conformation faults from occurring and minimize others.

The horse should also be trimmed to go barefoot any time shoes are removed and are not being put back on immediately. When winter comes and the horse is not to be used for a while or any time the horse is not to be ridden or used for a month or more, the shoes should be pulled and the horse allowed to go barefoot. This practice will provide for a much healthier foot that will be disease resistant, more resistant to wear and also hold a shoe on better when shoeing is necessary.

The first step in trimming or shoeing a horse is to remove the old shoes if they are still on. Proper removal of the shoes is important because it determines the condition the foot is left in after the removal. If the clinches are not loosened properly, chunks of the hoof can be pulled off with the shoe, leaving rough spots and gaps in the hoof wall. The clinch cutters work very well in preventing this by loosening the clinches so the shoe will come off easily.

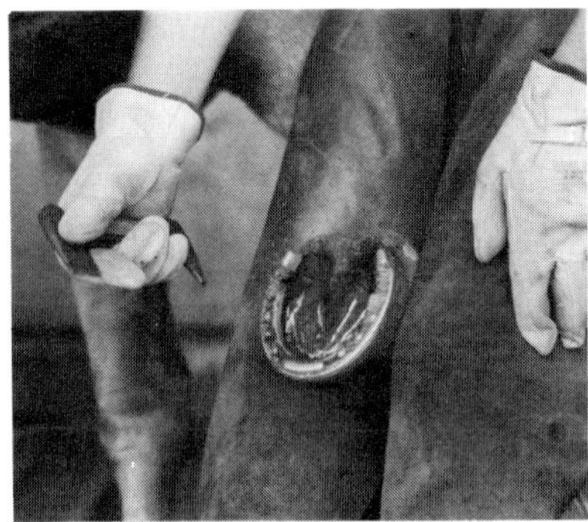

Fig 44. Foot in the shoeing position.

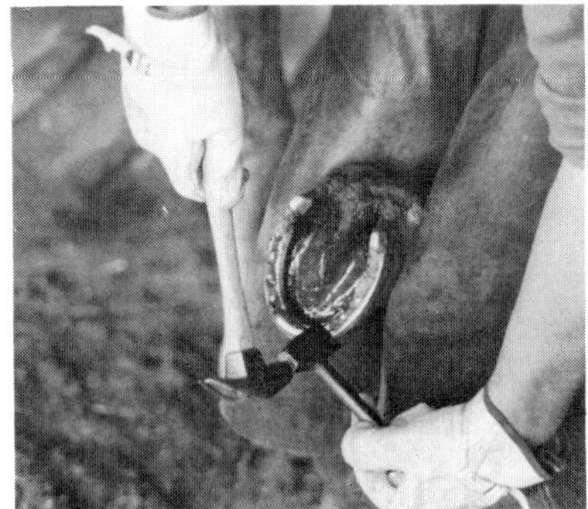

Fig 45. Mark the shoe.

Step 1- Bring the foot up into the shoeing position.

Step 1a- If the shoe is to be reused mark the shoe so that it can be put back on the corresponding foot. Suggestions for marking: Take the blade of the clinch cutters and place it on the shoe. Strike it with the hammer to leave a mark on the outside branch of the shoe as you are looking down on it. Strike it near the toe area if it is a front foot and near the heel if it is a rear foot. When you go to put the shoe back on a foot, make sure the mark is to the outside of the foot. (Outside here means furthest from the horse).

Step 2- Place the clinch cutter blade under a clinch.

Step 3- Strike the clinch cutter to remove or loosen the clinch. Repeat with all clinches.

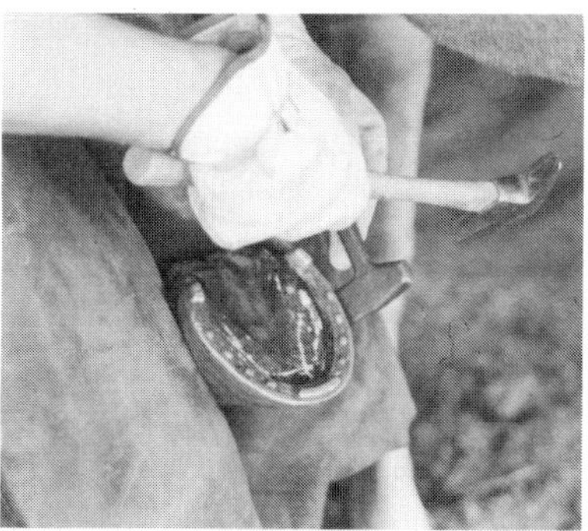

Fig 46. Strike the clinch cutter to loosen the clinch.

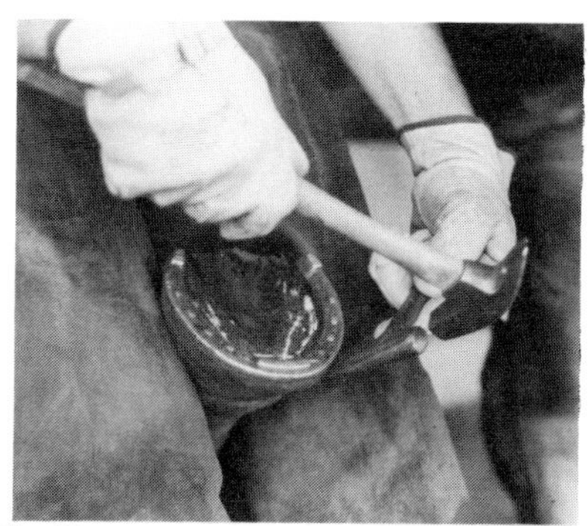

Fig 47.

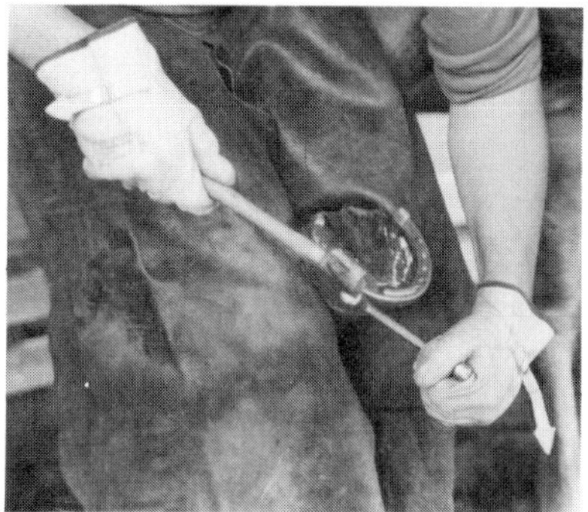

Fig 48.

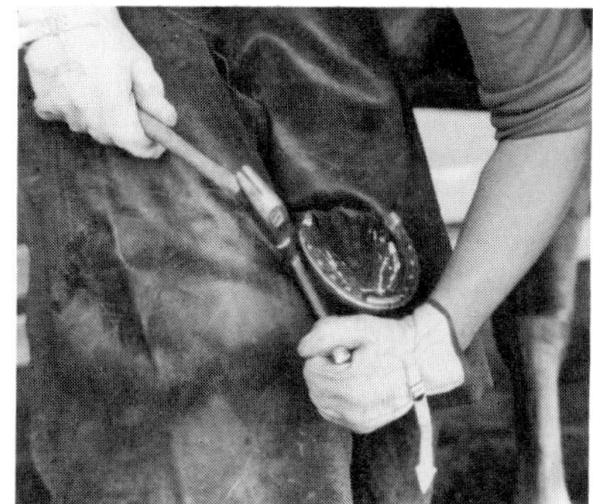

Fig 49.

Step 4- Place the shoe pulloff under the heel on one of the branches of the shoe.

Step 5- Gently push the pulloff handle towards the toe. The shoe should loosen some.

Step 6- Place the pulloffs under the opposite heel and push towards the toe. *Note: It is important that the toe of the foot is*

Step 7- Repeat as necessary, alternating sides until each branch is loose and the shoe comes off.

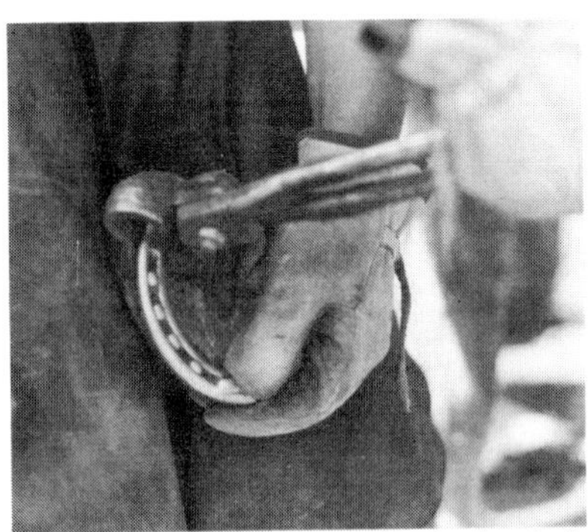

Fig 50. Place pulloffs under the heel of the shoe.

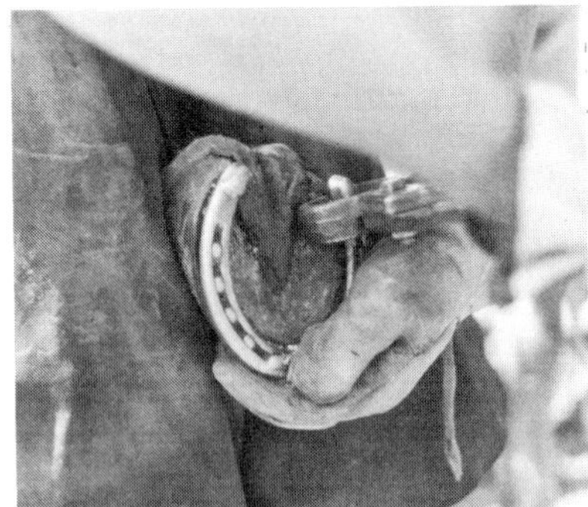

Fig 51. Support the toe as you push the pulloffs toward the toe.

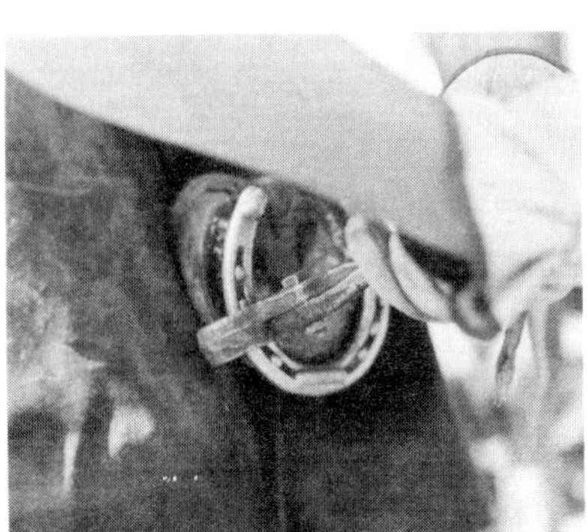

Fig 52. Repeat as necessary alternating sides.

Fig 53. Until each branch is loose or the shoe comes off.

TRIMMING

Step 1- Look at the horse's foot on a flat, level surface. Decide before beginning what needs to be done to balance the foot. Does the foot point to one side or the other? If so then the side it is pointing towards will need a little more hoof wall taken off. If the toes are pointing in then the inside hoof wall should be trimmed (no more than 1/8" lower than the other side.) An imaginary line drawn through the center of the pastern should approximate the angle through the hoof.

Under normal circumstances the toe will need to be cut more than the heels. This is mainly due to the fact that the hoof at the toe grows faster than the hoof at the heel. The most common mistake made is to cut too much heel off when trimming thereby breaking the angle back and putting extreme pressure on the flexor tendons. For the purpose of horseowners doing their own horses, only cut the toe. If anything is to be done to the heels use the rasp to level them.

Fig 54. Look at the foot (Before)

Fig 55. Check angle through pastern and hoof (Before)

Fig 56. Look at foot (After)

Fig 57. Check angle (After)

Step 2- Using the hoof knife trim away the "dead" sole. *The knife must be held in the palm of the hand so that the sharp edge is facing you.* Use the curved point of the hoof knife to do the trimming. The dead sole is dull and flaky as opposed to the live sole which is shiny and smooth. Trim the sole only until the composition of the sole changes from dull to shiny. If the area begins to look pink or red, stop trimming immediately, you have gone too far! Only trim the sole around the toe area within 1/4" of the white line. The only reason for trimming the sole at all is to find out how far to trim back the excess hoof wall. The rest of the dead sole on the bottom of the foot should be left to wear away naturally and serve as protection for the foot. When trimming to go barefoot, only cut away enough sole to provide a groove for the nippers. Remember more hoof wall and sole needs to be left on when going barefoot.

Step 3- Trim the bars back to the level of the sole. This is done to prevent them from growing too long, forming a false sole, or from breaking off and possibly causing lameness.

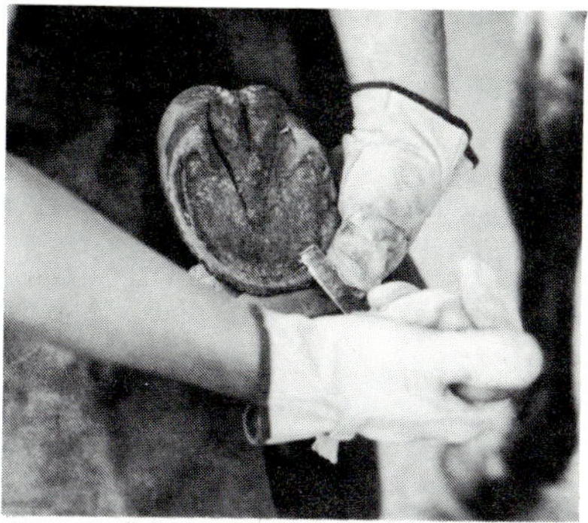

Fig 58. Trim away the dead sole. Note the proper way to hold the knife

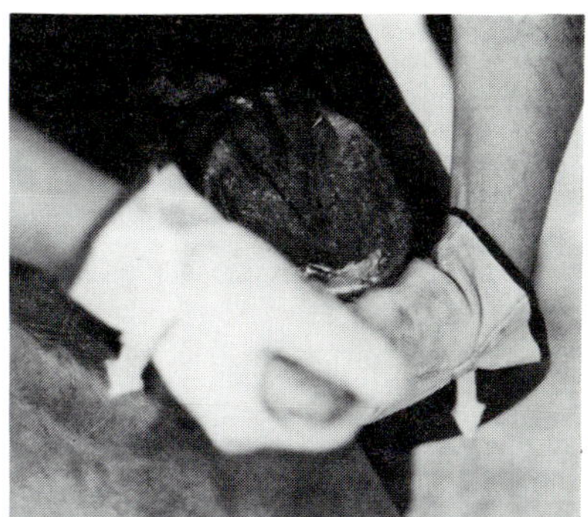

Fig 59. Trim within 1/4" of the white line

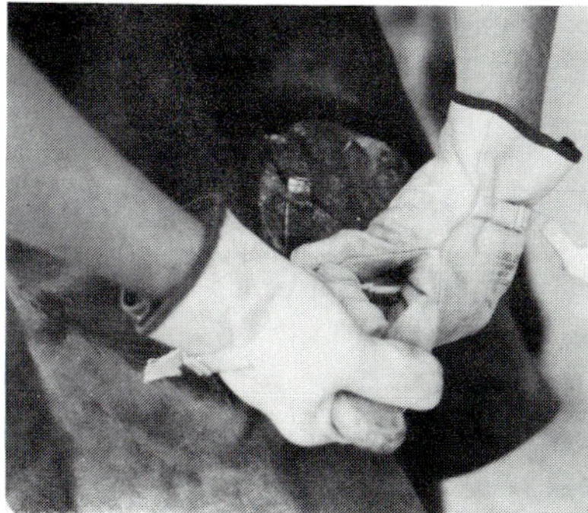

Fig 60. Trim the bar back to the level of the sole

Fig 61. Trim the bar back to the level of the sole

Step 4- Pare away any ragged or diseased part of the frog. Other than that, leave the frog alone. It serves a very important function (see anatomy section).

Step 5- Insert the hoof nippers at the toe to the level of the knife groove. Be sure the nippers are cutting perpendicular to the bearing surface of the hoof.

Beginning at the center of the toe, overlap each nipper cut approximately one-half of the nipper edge. Gradually bring each cut towards the heel so that by the time the quarters are reached the nipper cuts are through the excess hoof wall.

Step 6- Take the rasp to trim the quarters and heel area. Use the fine side of the rasp on the quarters since they are extremely soft and it is very easy to take off too much and make a serious mistake. The sole is lower at the quarters making the hoof wall seem higher. Be very careful not to cut the wall too low at the quarters. This is the reason only the rasp should be used at this section by beginners. Rasp only one side at a time and avoid "bouncing" the rasp on the near side. Rasp from heel to toe in long even strokes. Only rasp the high spots and continually check to see if it is level and balanced. If a mistake is made and part of the hoof is too low, don't compound the problem by continuing to rasp around it. Learn from the mistake and try to do better next time.

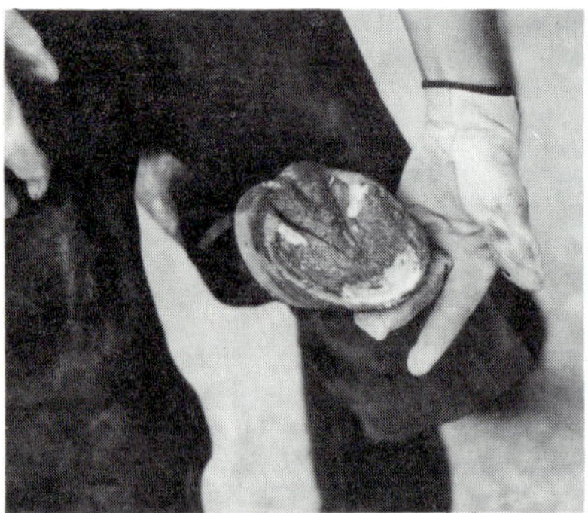

Fig 62. Foot ready for nipper cut

Fig 63. Insert nipper at the toe - overlap each cut

Fig 64. Rasp with long, even strokes

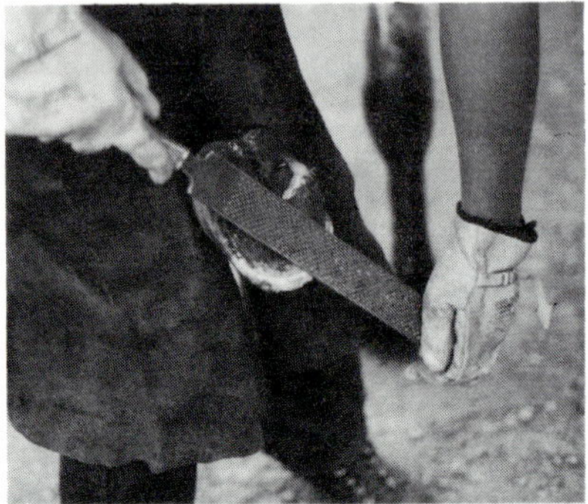

Fig 65. Rasp with long even strokes

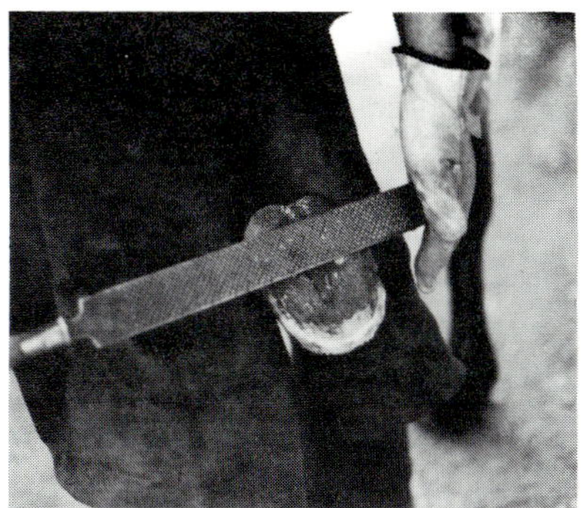

Fig 66. Rasp one side at a time

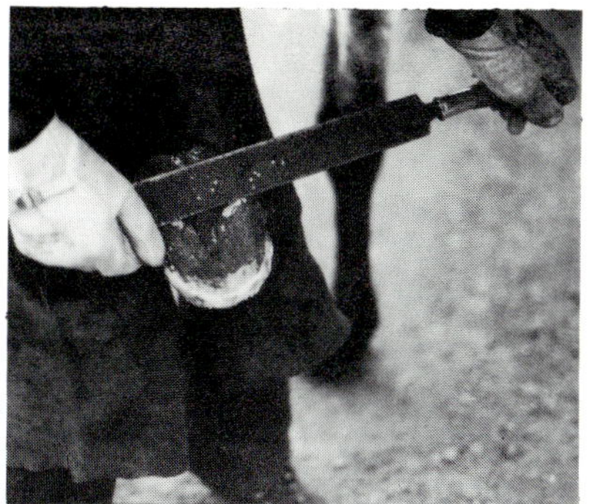

Fig 67. Avoid "bouncing" the rasp on the near side

Step 7- Take the nippers and using the A-B line as a guide, nipper the hoof wall edge at a 45 degree angle above the A-B line. Take off approximately 1/2 the width of the hoof wall with the nippers. This step is done to help the beginner to determine how much of the foot is to be rasped while rounding the edges.

Step 8- Bring the foot up and put it on a stand (or the lap). Take the rasp and round the edges left from the 45 degree nipper cut. This is to keep the hoof from chipping while the horse is barefoot. Continue to round the hoof wall back to the heels.

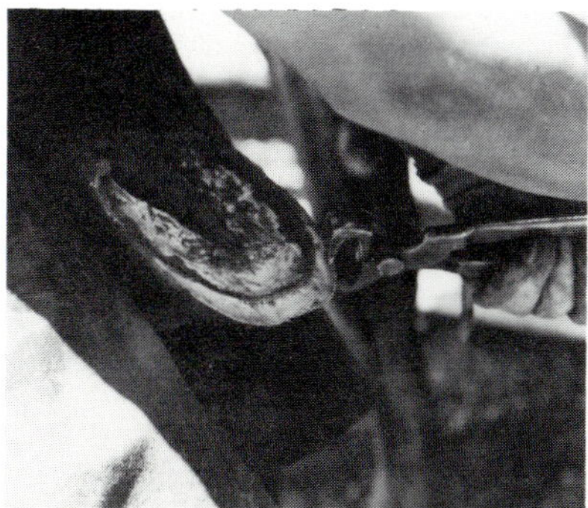

Fig 68. Nipper the hoof wall edge at a 45° angle

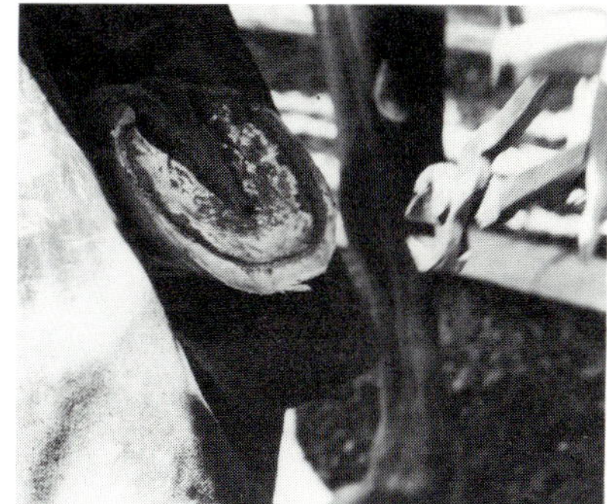

Fig 69. Nipper approximately 1/2 the width of the hoof wall

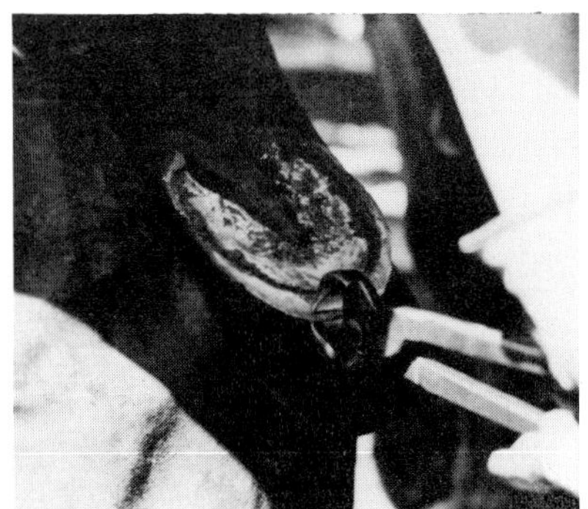

Fig 70. Nipper around the toe

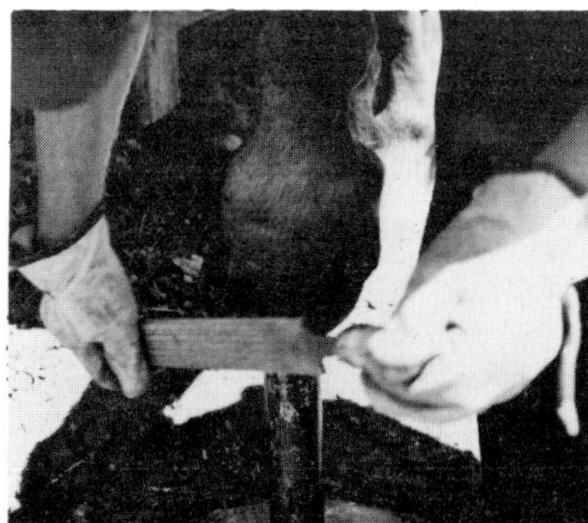

Fig 71. Put the foot on the stand

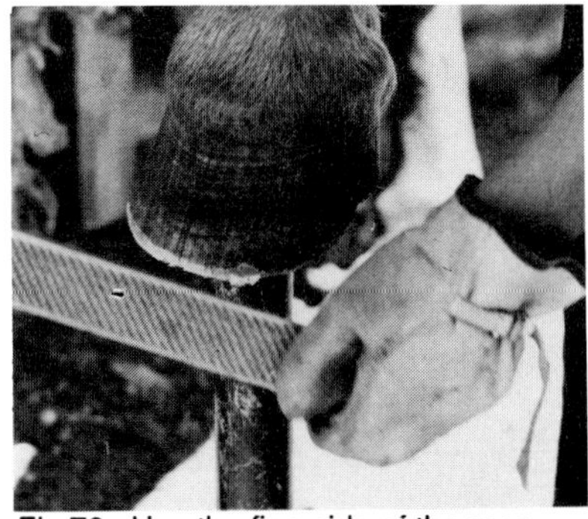

Fig 72. Use the fine side of the rasp

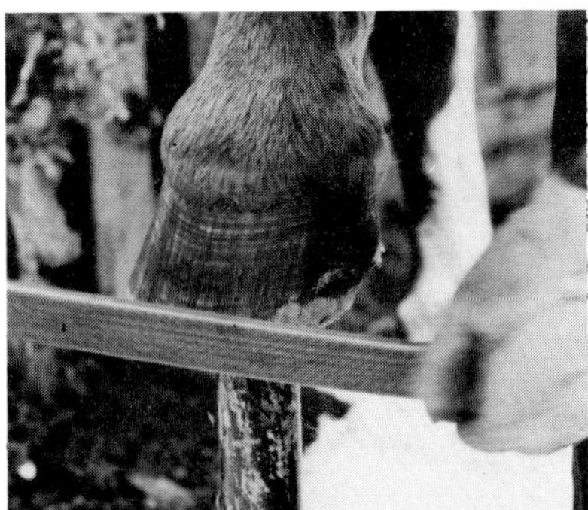

Fig 73. Round the edges of the hoof wall back to the heels

Note: Steps 7 and 8 are not required when shoeing the horse.

Step 9- The foot should also be balanced and any obvious flaring taken off. When rasping flares it is important to not just chop it off at a 90 degree angle. Blend the flares into the natural angle of the hoof wall.

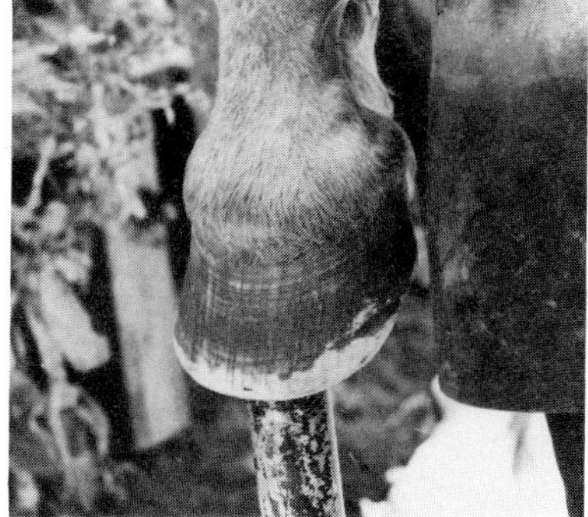

Fig 74. Any obvious flares should be taken off

Fig 75. Blend the flares into the natural angle of the hoof wall

=== NOTES ===

SHOEING

Begin preparing the foot for shoeing by trimming the foot.

The basic steps for barefoot trimming still apply with the exception that the hoof wall will be shortened as much as practical to allow room for the extra weight and length of the shoe. The steps involving the 45 degree angle cut to round the sharp outer edge (Steps 7 & 8) are not required. A rasp should be run around the edge, however, just enough to remove the sharp edge. This will help prevent cuts on the hands.

Before shaping the shoe, be sure the foot has been brought forward and any flares removed. Make sure the foot is balanced and composed to the best extent.

Fitting the Shoe- The shoe must fit the hoof. This means that the hoof should never be rasped off once the shoe has been nailed on. *In theory and practice, for a competent farrier, this is true. However, for the beginner, one who lacks skill in shaping and balancing a hoof, this rule can be bent. However, if any hoof is to be rasped off, it must be done following the angle of the hoof. Do not club the toe off at a 90 degree angle.*

Diagram 3. Front Foot

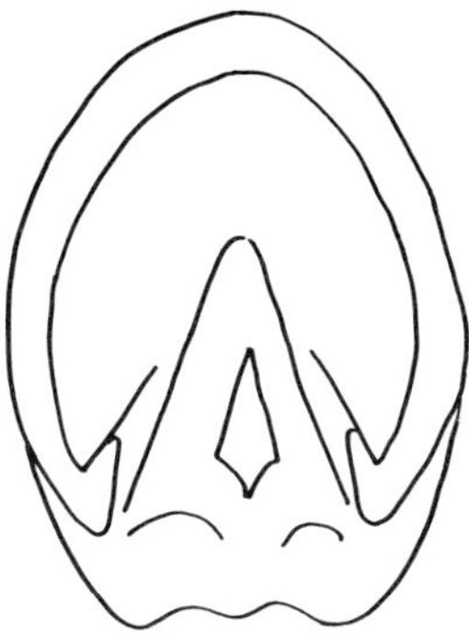

Diagram 4. Hind Foot

When fitting a shoe to the hoof, the outside edge of the shoe should fit exactly the outside edge of the hoof wall at the toe and quarters. From the last nail hole back to the buttress of the heel, the shoe should stick out approximately the width of a nickel. In other words, a nickel should be able to be rolled along the edge of the shoe from the last nail hole back.

(Author's Note:

When fitting the shoe, a beginner can use the white line as a guide to help determine what the hoof should look like. The hoof will undergo changes because of environment, faulty shoeing or conformation. The white line will determine the shape of the hoof. The coffin bone is the basis of the shape of the foot; the white line is the mechanism that holds the hoof wall to the coffin bone and hence is the determining factor in the true shape of the hoof wall. When shaping the shoe to the wall, especially in a neglected foot, the white line can be used to help shape it. The nail holes are put in the shoe to correspond to the white line.

Each nail is to be driven into the outer edge of the white line. Therefore if the nail holes line up over the white line, then the shoe should fit properly and excess hoof wall can be rasped off after the shoe is nailed on. This is best done after 2 nails have been driven and before all nails are put in.

When rasping the hoof wall, keep in mind the rules for rasping off flares. Rasp only in a line with the natural angle of the hoof wall. Do not chop off the excess in a 90 degree angle. Rasp only the bottom 1 1/2 - 2" of the hoof. Do not rasp near the hair line.)

Once the shoe is properly fitted it is ready to be nailed on.

NAILS AND NAILING

Nails come in sizes approximately 1/4" difference in length. Therefore a #4 nail is 1/4" shorter than a #5 nail. Nails also come in different head styles. The most common are Regular and Cityhead. The nail most commonly used for saddle horse shoeing is the #5 Cityhead. This nail works well with #00, #0, and #1 sized shoes. If a #2 or larger shoe is used a #5 Regular head will work better. The difference in the heads is that the Cityhead is a smaller head for use in smaller shoes and the Regular head is a larger head for use in larger shoes and for resetting smaller shoes. *(Author's note: After 8-10 weeks on a horse's hoof, the crease portion of the shoe (where the nail heads set) will open up and flatten out causing a larger nail head to be needed in order to seat properly.)*

It is desirable to use the smallest nail that will sufficiently hold the shoe to the foot. Every nail driven into the horse's foot does some damage. The ideal is to do the least amount of damage. Using the proper size nail, a properly fitted shoe and proper nailing techniques will help accomplish this.

The nails have a beveled point which helps the nail curve in order to come out of the hoof when driven. The flat side of the nail head is always to go to the outside of the shoe. The tapered part of the head must always be towards the inside of the foot. The tapered part of the nail has a design on it that can be felt. Always check before driving the nail that it is turned the proper way. If turned the wrong way it would curve towards the sensitive structures rather than away and out of the hoof.

Driving the nails into the horse's hoof is a great concern to beginners. It is the most dangerous part of horseshoeing as far as potential damage to the horse. If the directions that follow are adhered to it will be virtually impossible to drive a bad nail and do permanent damage to the horse.

**Note the rectangular shape
of the nail holes. (see step 4)**

Step 1- The shoe must be properly shaped (see section on fitting shoe) so that the nail holes are over the white line.

Step 2- Select the proper size nails.

Step 3- Before each nail is placed in the nail hole make sure the flat edged side is pointed away from the hoof center and the trademark or design side is pointed in.

Step 4- The nail holes in the shoe are rectangular in shape. The flat side of the nail must be contacting the outside edge of the nail hole. The nail must also be centered in the hole from front to back. In addition, the nail must be driven perpendicular to the shoe. If not, the shoe will shift on the foot either frontwards or more likely backwards off the toe. In fact, with the natural tendency of driving nails towards the body which would promote the shoe sliding off the toe, it is best to point the nail slightly forward to offset this.

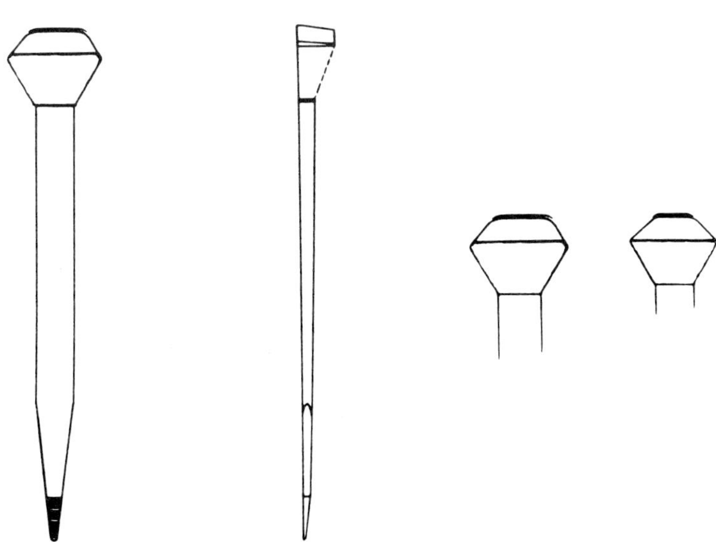

Diagram 5.

Step 5- The next step is driving the nail. The object is to get two nails in the shoe before the horse has a chance to jerk his foot away or the horseowner becomes too tired to hold the foot up. It is recommended that the second nail hole from the toe on each side is used. This is a fairly easy place in the hoof to get a nail to come out properly. It is also fairly easy to adjust the shoe if it slips when driving the first nail. Once these nails are in and holding the shoe in place, the more important heel nails can be driven. *(Author's note: The heel nails are important because they do more to hold the shoe on. If a shoe is to pull off too soon, it is usually because of it pulling from the heel. In addition the last nail on each side has no other nail to help it whereas at the toe each nail is supported from two sides. Therefore take time with the heel nails and put in good nails at the proper height.)*

Drive the nail to the side of the hammer hand first (right-handed persons will drive the right side nail first and left-handed persons vice versa). This will allow the use of the off hand to help hold the shoe as well as put in the nail. Drive the nail about half an inch. This will help hold the shoe in position.

Step 6- Adjust the shoe as necessary. Put in a nail on other side and drive it through the hoof aiming it to come out 3/4" high. Nail at least half way and determine if it is coming out yet. If it is, good. If not, try driving it another 1/4". If still not coming out, pull the nail and try another nail. If the time is taken to check each nail as it is being driven it will be hard to drive a nail that doesn't come out. Drive the nail through the hoof. Make sure the nail head is seated in the hole by hitting it at least once when it is in the crease. Immediately bend the exposed part of the nail over with the driving hammer.

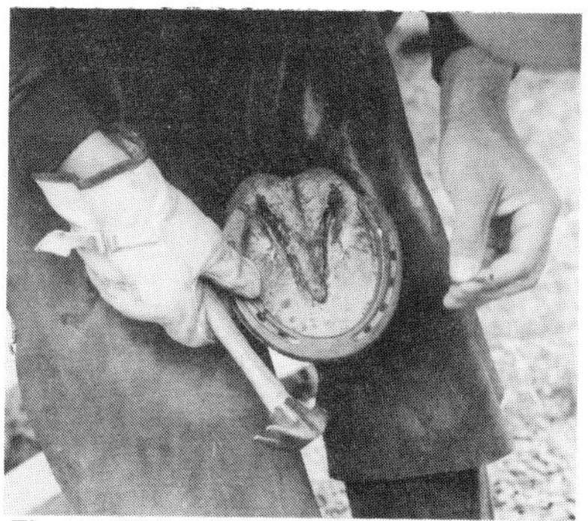

Fig 76. Drive the first nail to the hammer side

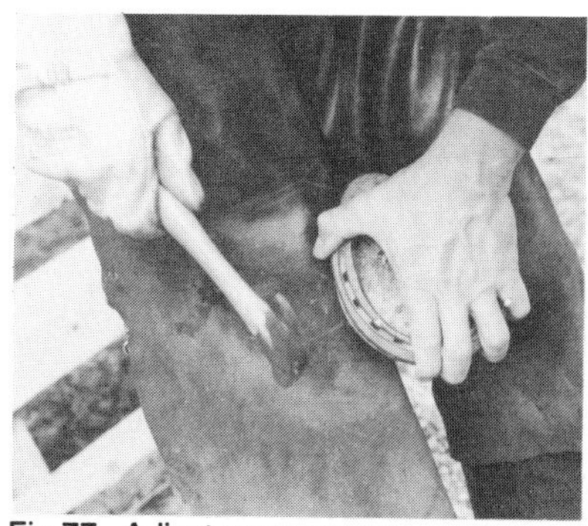

Fig 77. Adjust as necessary

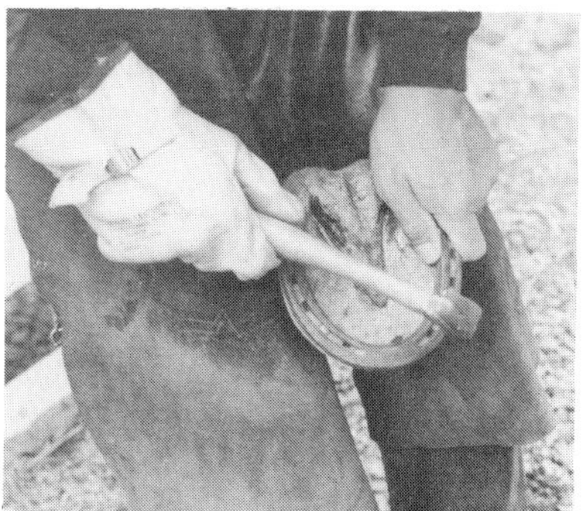

Fig 78. Drive the nail through the hoof

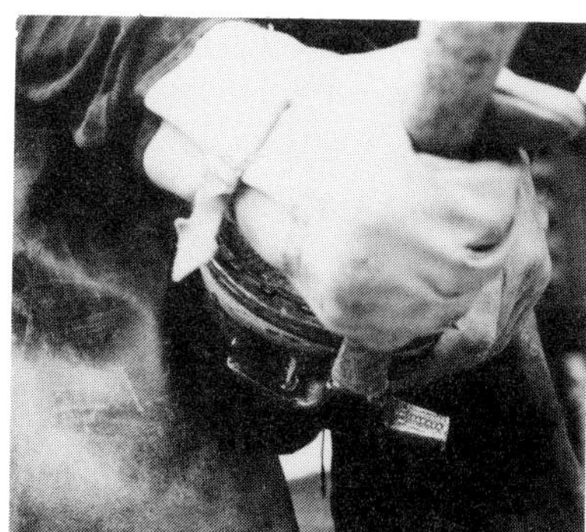

Fig 79. Immediately bend nail over

Step 7- Return to the first nail and drive it through (after adjusting the shoe if necessary). Make sure the head is seated, then bend over the exposed part of the nail with the driving hammer.

Step 8- Put the foot on the ground and check to see if the shoe still looks like it fits properly. Does it fit at the toe, at the quarter and is there proper expansion (approximately the width of a nickel edge from the last nail hole back) in the heel area? The shoe looks different when it is on the ground and a shoe that is not shaped properly will show itself now. It is easier to pull the shoe with only 2 nails in it than to wait until all nails have been put in to discover the shoe doesn't fit. Always look at the foot after two nails have been driven!!! If the shoe needs to be removed, simply cut the exposed nails with the nail nippers and use the shoe pulloff to pull the shoe.

Step 9- Drive the rest of the nails alternating from one side to the other. On smaller feet (00,0,1) that are in good condition six nails will hold the shoe adequately. Leave the last nails out of each side to allow for heel expansion (optional).

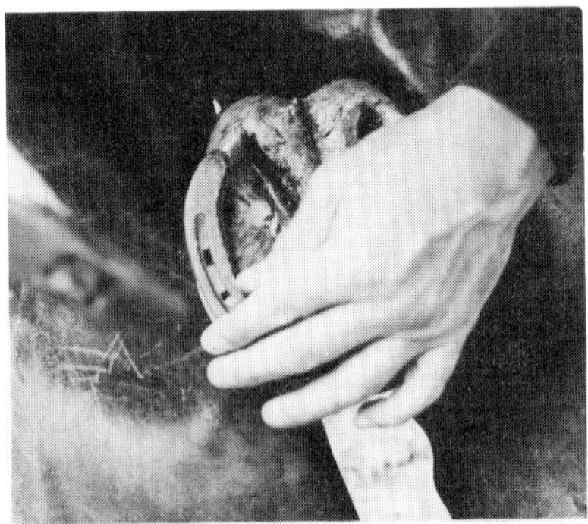

Fig 80. Drive the nail through the hoof

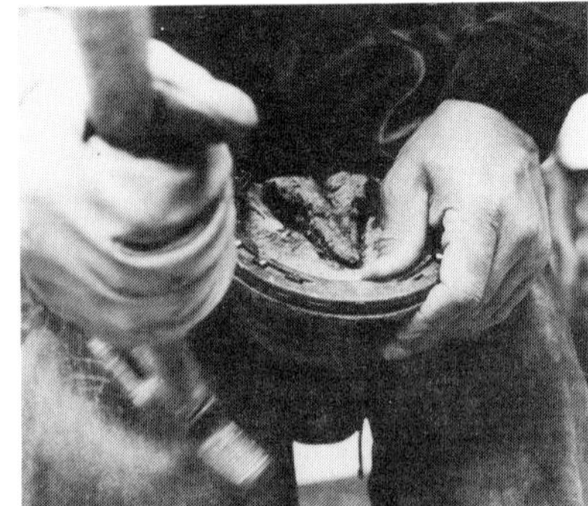

Fig 81. Fold nail over with hammer

Fig 82. Put the foot on the ground

Fig 83. Drive the rest of the nails

S t e p 10- Check the nails. Are they all about 3/4" high? If one is too high or too low, now is the time to fix it.

Pull the nail and redrive it or use another open nail hole. Remember the importance of the heel nail. If the last nail is not a very good one, it would be better to use the vacant nail hole left for ease of expansion than to risk losing the shoe too soon due to a bad nail.

In order to make a nail come out sooner, the point can be bent slightly thereby allowing the nail to drive out sooner. This can be done with the shoeing hammer. Use this when the nails are coming out too high or not at all.

There are several ways to remove a nail head from the crease. The easiest is using a crease nail puller. It is possible to loosen the head enough so it can be pulled by one of two methods.

Method 1- Cut the exposed nail off, hammer the stub perpendicular to the wall, place clinching block or rasp under stub, and strike the shoe next to the head with the hammer.

Method 2- Cut the exposed nail off, place point of clinch cutter under nail and strike with hammer.

Quicking or Close Nailing

If, despite carefully following the above directions on nailing, the horse is "quicked" there is something that can be done. Quicking can be recognized if the horse jerks its foot, if there is a change of the sound of the driving nail or if blood is coming from the hole. If this happens, remove the nail and do not use that hole again this shoeing. Treat the hole with 7% iodine solution or similar treatment and get the horse a tetanus booster. Without complications the horse should be fine.

<hr>

NOTES

CLINCHING

Clinching is the process whereby the nails are cut off and finished to properly hold the shoe on. Proper clinching is one of the variables that help determine how long the shoeing job will last. The tools needed for clinching are the driving hammer, the clinch block, the rasp and the nail nippers.

Step 1- Pick the foot up in the shoeing position. Under each exposed part of the nail place the clinch block or side of a rasp. Lightly tap each corresponding nail head with the hammer. This insures that the head is seated and tightens the nail in the foot. Do not hit too hard or the exposed nail will pull through the hoof wall. Alternate tightening from side to side as when driving the nails.

Fig 84. Foot with all nails driven and folded over - ready for clinching

Fig 85. Place clinch block under each nail

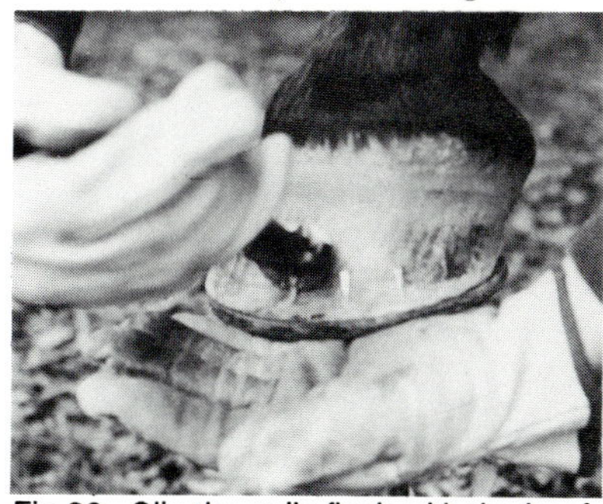
Fig 86. Clip the nails flush with the hoof

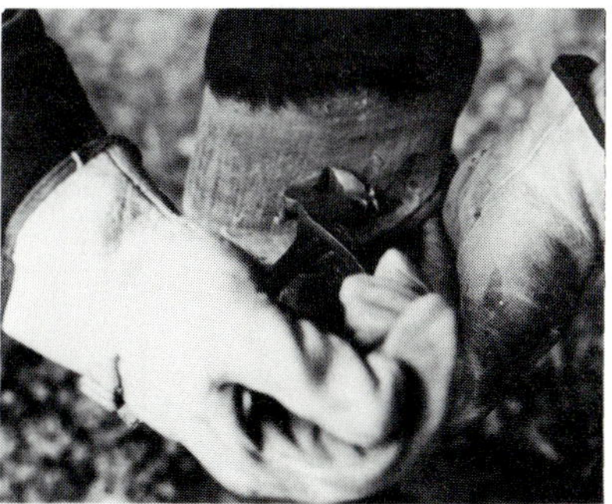
Fig 87. Clip the nails flush with the hoof

Step 2- Bring the foot forward on the stand and clip the nails flush with the hoof with the nail nippers.

Step 3- Take the edge of the rasp and lightly file the hoof material under each nail. This forms a slight pocket for each nail to bend into when clinched.

Step 4- Take the clinching tongs and clinch each nail. Let the clinchers do the work. Squeeze the handle together; don't wrench the tool down. This will cause ripping of the hoof wall.

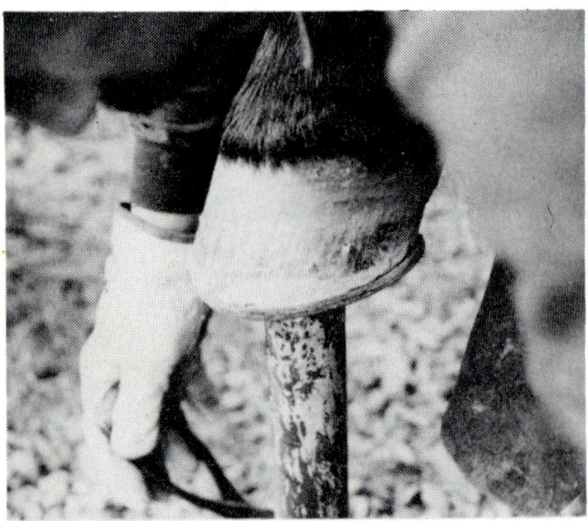

Fig 88. Nails clipped flush with the hoof

Fig 89. Use the fine side of the rasp

Fig 90. Lightly file under each nail

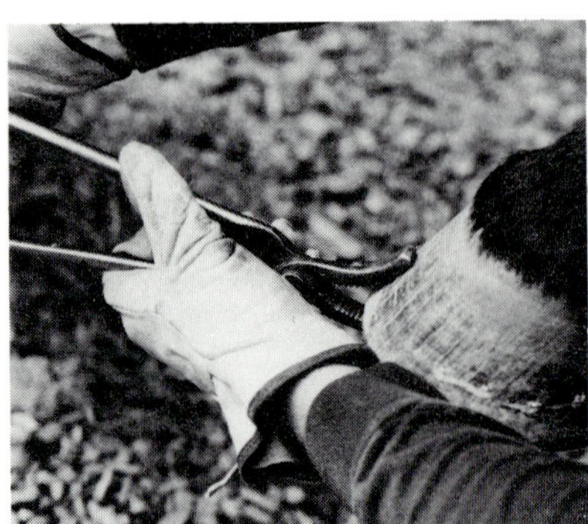

Fig 91. Use clinchers to clinch nail

Step 5- Finish each clinch with the hammer and clinch block or rasp. Place the clinch block under a nail head and strike the clinch with the hammer directly toward the hoof.

Step 6- Take the fine side of the rasp and lightly file each clinch to take away any rough edges. This will help prevent injury to the horseowner or horse if the clinches are rubbed.

Fig 92. Clinch each nail

Fig 93. Use hammer and clinch block to finish nails

Fig 94. Lightly file each clinch to take off any rough edges

HORSESHOES

There are many different types, styles, and manufacturers of horseshoes. Under ideal conditions, the best shoe to use would be a hand made shoe from a length of bar stock. The advantage of this type of shoe is that the weight and the fit of the shoe, the position of the nail holes and the length of the heels of the shoe can all be exactly custom made for each individual foot. However this takes considerable skill and investment in equipment and is thus impractical for the horseowner.

Another type of shoe is a machine made "hot" shoe. This shoe is made with prepunched nail holes and with long heels that need to be cut off and finished as required for each foot. This shoe has the advantage of being able to be customized depending on the foot. Once again, however, a considerable investment in equipment makes it impractical for most horseowners.

Keg shoes or machine made shoes with the heels already finished are ideal for the type of shoeing intended in this book. They are available in nearly any style and size required. The shoes are generally made from mild steel and are work hardened. That is, the shoe is fairly easy to shape when it is new; however as the shoe gets worked on the anvil or as the horse pounds it on the ground for a while it will harden and become quite difficult to shape. This is one reason why resetting shoes is not recommended by the author. Since it is seldom that the horse's foot does not change from shoeing to shoeing, changes must be made in the shape of the shoe. With a shoe that has been hardened through wear, it is difficult to reshape it cold. It is recommended that new shoes be used each time.

A variation of the keg shoes is what is called "ready made". These shoes come in a front and a hind pattern (the front pattern being rounded and the hind pattern being pointed). These shoes can save the horseowner time and work since the major alteration has already been accomplished.

Shoes - Types

1) *Full swedged shoes* - have a crease that runs the full length of the shoe (toe, quarter, heel). This shoe is generally a lighter shoe and is used most often when the horse is to be used in arenas or on turf.

2) *Fullered* - the crease is only in the area of the nail holes. This is the most popular type of shoe and gives good all around wear.

3) *Counter sink* - the shoe is creased only at the nail hole. This type is generally only used when making a shoe from bar stock.

Styles

1) *Rim shoes* - the shoe is a full swedged shoe with equal length rims.

2) *Barrel race shoes* - the shoe is a full swedged shoe with the front rim higher than the rear rim.

3) *Polo shoe* - the shoe is a full swedged shoe with the rear rim higher that the front rim.

4) *Training plate shoe* - the shoe is a full swedged shoe. Essentially a thinner, lighter rim shoe.

5) *Plate shoe* - the shoe is a fullered shoe.

6) *Heeled shoe* - the shoe is a fullered shoe with ready made heel caulks.

7) *Toe and heeled shoe* - the shoe is a fullered shoe with ready made toe and heel caulks.

Shoe Selection

The factors which most commonly influence the style of shoe used are: the horseowner's preference, the type of work the horse will be doing, the type of ground the horse is being worked on and the price and local availability of the shoes. The author's preference is the plate or rim shoe. These shoes resemble the natural surface of the horse's foot and give good service for most conditions. The selection of the shoe should be based on what is best for the horse. As far as the physiological function of the horse's foot is concerned, a flat plate shoe is best. The shoe should be as light as possible and still be heavy enough to last the period between shoeings (8-10 weeks). The ground over which the horse is to be used need to be considered. The shoe needs to be wide enough to protect the hoof and heavy enough to last. The shoe width should be at least twice the thickness of the hoof wall. This is the minimum needed for adequate sole protection on a normal foot.

56   Horseshoeing for Horseowners

FITTING THE SHOE

Properly fitting and shaping the shoe may give beginners a great deal of trouble. It will be the most time consuming part in the beginning while learning where and how to hit the shoe to shape it. Since it is time consuming, many beginners will stop attempting to shape the shoe and begin to think, "It looks close enough to me". That is where the shoeing job will begin to break down. It is important that the shoe fit the foot. This chapter will demonstrate how to change the shape of the shoe to correspond to the shape of the foot.

In order to shape the shoe, the shape of the foot must be known first. Look at the foot, at the outside edge of the hoof wall on a properly prepared foot. What does the foot look like? Is the toe round, flat or pointed? Are the quarters rounded or straight? How much do the heels

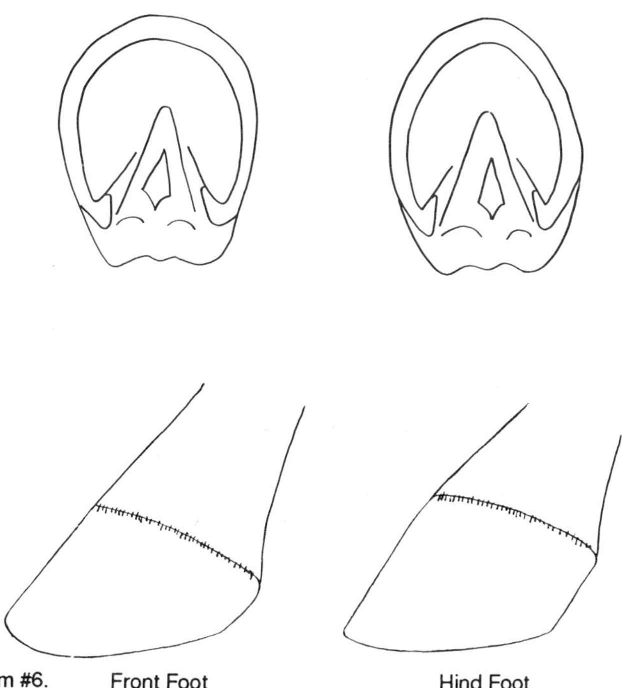

Diagram #6.   Front Foot   Hind Foot

turn? Is each half of the foot the same or is one half shaped slightly different? (It is common to have the inside half straighter in the quarters than the outside half) Only when the general shape of the foot is known, is the shoe brought to the foot.

Does the shoe look like it will fit the foot? The buttress of each heel must be covered. Will the shoe still fit the heels after it has been shaped? Remember the smallest, lightest shoe that will properly cover the foot is the one to use. The shoe must cover the buttress of the heel or corns, bruises or even heel breakage can result.

Once the shape of the foot is known and the size of the shoe is selected, then the shoe may be shaped. Start shaping the shoe from the toe to the quarters to the heel. Make the toe of the shoe look like the toe of the foot. Make the quarters of the shoe look like the quarters of the foot. Make the heels of the shoe look like the heels of the foot. If the shape of the foot is forgotten, go to the horse and look again, but do not put the shoe on the foot. The only time the shoe should be put on the foot is for final fitting, checking for expansion. What can happen is that the shoe will be put on the foot to see what doesn't fit. Then the shoe will be changed accordingly and put back on the foot to check.

Each time something is changed on the shoe it changes another part of the shoe. Unless the general shape of the shoe is the same as the general shape of the foot, the shoe will never fit. Avoid doing it by feel, bit by bit. This I call the "Braille" method and seldom works. Make the shoe look like the foot in the toe first, round, flat or pointed. Then make the quarters of the shoe look like the quarters of the foot--straight, round, etc. Then make the heel of the shoe look like the heel of the foot. Then if the shoe overall looks like the foot, take the shoe to the foot. All that needs to be done now is to check to see if the shoe is too narrow or too wide for the foot.

SHAPING THE SHOE

All alterations of the shoe can be done by mastering a few basic principles.

To Round the Toe- Place the shoe over the horn or heel of the anvil. The more space allowed between the shoe and the anvil, the more the toe will be rounded. Hit the shoe over the center of the toe.

To Point the Toe- Place one branch of the shoe over the heel. Depending on the size of the shoe or the width of the heel of the anvil, the shoe may need to be opened first. Strike the shoe as close to the center of the toe as possible. This will straighten the shoe at that point. Repeat this procedure with the other branch. Then close the shoe. This will point the toe of the shoe.

Fig 95. Round the toe

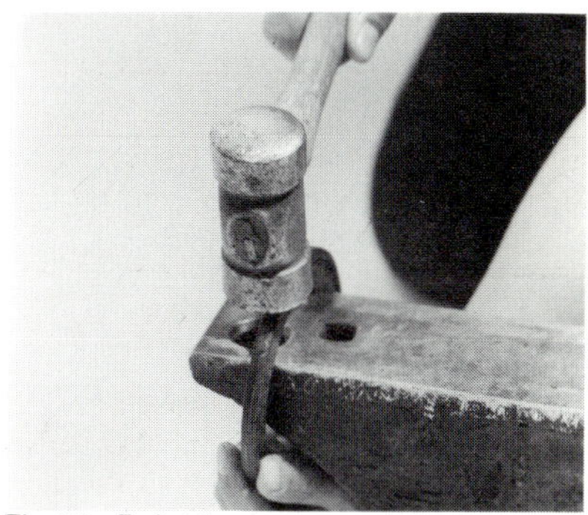
Fig 96. Point the toe

To Open the Shoe- Place the shoe branches equally over the edge of the anvil and strike the center of the toe.

To Close the Shoe- Hold the shoe at the toe and place it over the anvil as shown. Strike the shoe directly on the branch.

To Straighten the Quarter- Place the shoe over the heel of the anvil much like when pointing the toe. However, to straighten the quarter, the branch must be over the anvil. Strike the shoe at the point where the shoe needs to be straightened.

To Round the Quarter- This can be accomplished in two ways. The branch can be placed over the horn where the shoe needs to be rounded. As the shoe is being struck, the shoe should be pulled around the horn. The hammer should strike the shoe just off the point where it meets the anvil. If this is not done the shoe will tend to "jump" out of the hand holding it.

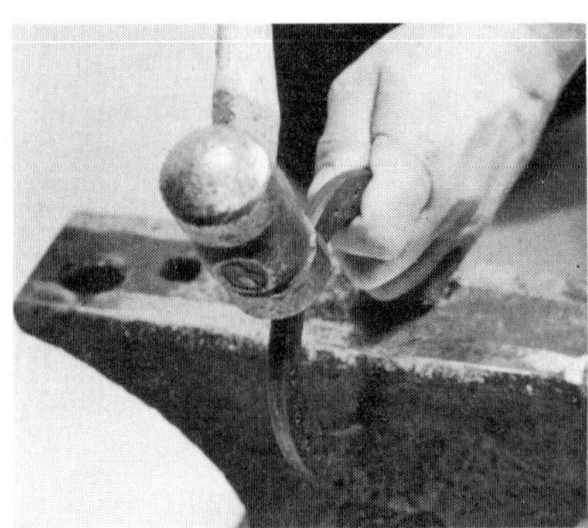

Fig 97. Open the shoe

Fig 98. Close the shoe

Fig 99. Straighten the quarter

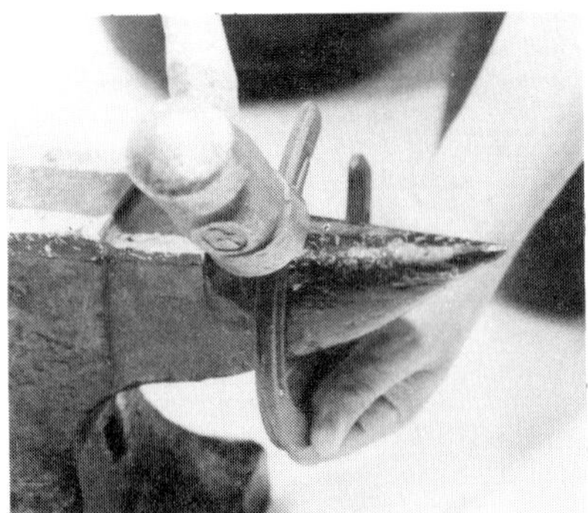

Fig 100. Round the quarter

An easier way to accomplish this for beginners is to place the quarters of the shoe up through the hardy hole. Strike the shoe near the heel to get the quarters to round.

To Turn the Heels In- This can be accomplished in the same ways as rounding the quarters. The difference is in where the shoe is placed and hit. To turn the heels the shoe must be struck closer to the heels, then up the quarters.

To Straighten the Heel- Place the heel of the shoe over the heel of the anvil. Strike the shoe at the point that the heel must be straightened.

Fig 101. Round the quarter using the hardy hole

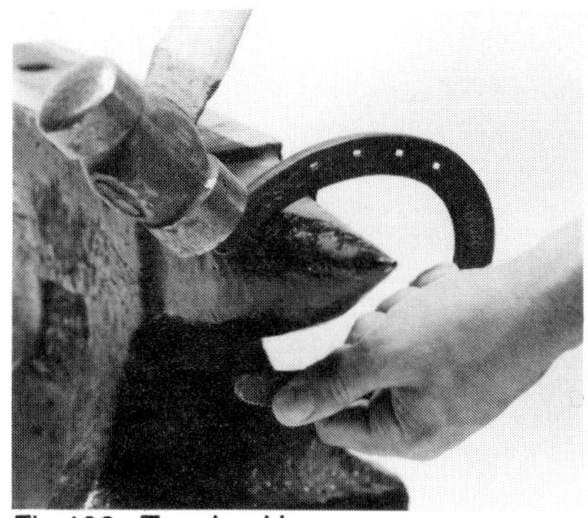

Fig 102. Turn heel in

Fig 103. Turn heel in with hardy hole

Fig 104. Straighten the heel

To Open One Side of the Shoe- This must be done sometimes because one side of the foot is larger than the other. Place the branch that needs to be extended over the edge of the anvil with the other branch placed perpendicular to the anvil. Strike the shoe at the toe.

Leveling the Shoe- As the shoe is being struck to shape it, it is also being warped out of level. Since one of the keys to a good shoeing job is a level shoe on a level foot, the shoe must be kept level during the shaping.

Place the shoe on the anvil with the foot surface up. Strike overlapping blows on the inner surface of the shoe from the toe to one heel. Do the same to the other branch of the shoe. Place the shoe in the palm of one hand and hold it at arm's length. Sight across the branches to check if it is level. If not, place the shoe back on the anvil and strike as before on the high spots. Occasionally the shoe gets warped so much that it must be hit on the ground surface. Try to keep the shoe level as the shaping is taking place and it will be easier to level than to let it get out of level greatly and try to bring it back.

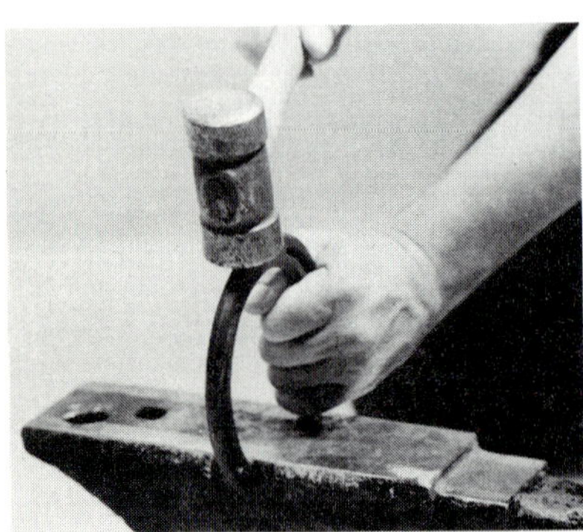

Fig 105. Open one side

Fig 106. Level shoe

Fig 107. Level shoe

Fig 108. Hold at arms length

HOW TO FIND A FARRIER

Even if you are one of the few who will shoe your own horse after reading this book, there are still times when you will want a farrier. I suggest that you have a professional do your horse at least once a year. This will insure that the feet are healthy and being trimmed and shod properly. It will also give you a chance to work with and learn from a professional.

Here are some suggestions for finding a competent farrier:

1) ask fellow horse owners for names of some shoers with whom they are happy.

2) ask your veterinarian

3) check the classifieds

4) check bulletin boards at farm and stores, etc.

Once you have some names to call there are some questions you want to ask. When the farrier arrives:

1) Is he on time?

2) Does he take time to question you about your horse? Questions like:

a) What are you going to be doing with it?

b) Does the horse have any old injuries that might affect the shoeing job?

c) Does the horse have any predisposition to travel faults?

3) Does he take time to observe the horse in motion?

4) Does he keep a file card on the horse showing things like shoe size and date of service?

Observe the shoer while he works. Is he following the basic principles of horseshoeing? The steps involved are not important. Everybody does it a little different. But the basic principles should not vary. If something is being done you don't understand, ask why. No competent farrier should mind being asked why he is doing something. Be wary of the farrier who doesn't want you around. He may have something to hide!!!

Some questions for the farrier:

1) What are your rates?

2) Where did you get your training? (I recommend a graduate of an accredited shoeing school)

3) Are you capable of corrective shoeing?

4) Are you fully equipped for corrective shoeing if necessary--forge, acrylics, pads, etc.?

5) Are you a full-time horseshoer?

(Author's note: I feel that in order to do a professional job, to keep up with advances, a farrier should do nothing but shoeing. Besides, if you need something done in an emergency, the chances are better that a full-time farrier could fit you in rather than have to work around another full time job.

6) How much lead time do you normally need to set up an appointment?

7) How do you handle emergency calls?

8) Are you familiar with my particular type of horse breed and particular use? (hunter, jumper, work, etc.)